Go Ahead—
Take the Wheel

Racing on Your Budget

by

Dave Grar

D1445611

Library of Congress Control Number: 2006901395
ISBN 13: 978-0-9777860-0-8
Front cover photo by Gene Rosintoski
copyright 2006
Roz Rosintoski Motorsports Photography
www.rozphoto.com

Dragon Publishing
copyright © David Gran, 2006
Printed in the United States of America
Go Ahead – Take the Wheel is also available at discounts in bulk quantity.
For details, write to Dragon Publishing, 15 Oxford Drive, Suite 315, Newington, CT 06111 USA or e-mail Contact@GoAheadTakeTheWheel.com.

Table of Contents

Prologue

I am often amused by the high costs that people claim are necessary to club race. When I hear people wanting to get involved in racing seek advice, these high cost estimates change from amusing to frustrating. Often potential racers become discouraged, believing they cannot afford to race. This was one of my primary motivations for writing this book. I was misled about the costs and other hurdles involved in racing, and I therefore put aside my racing dreams for several years. There are also people who have the financial resources to race, but simply don't know how to make racing a reality. Looking back now, it would have been beneficial to have had a resource to aid me in the pursuit of racing and to provide guidance about what it really takes to club race. This book will guide you in achieving your racing dreams on a wide range of financial budgets.

Racing is often referred to as a rich man's sport, but it certainly does not have to be. Before beginning my racing career, I spoke with many drivers while at various events as a spectator about how I could begin racing. I was shocked to hear that it could very easily cost $1,500 to race a single weekend event. Many people even told me that $1,500 would be a cheap weekend. This led to my next question. How much would it cost for a racecar? The answer for an "entry level" racecar started at $8,000 and quickly went up from there. At first I thought I was just asking the wrong people, so I continued talking with other drivers about the associated costs. I would walk away dejected thinking about the "cheap race weekend" and how there was no way I could afford to race at these costs. Needless to say, after a while I began to believe that this was the reality, which started to tear away at my dreams of racing. Some of my friends who also grew up dreaming about racing, told me that I just need to accept things as they are – you need to be born into racing or be very wealthy. I continued attending races and sat on the sidelines watching others do what I dreamed of doing for a few more years. I kept thinking that someday I would figure out how to begin racing.

One year I joined the Sports Car Club of America (SCCA). For some crazy reason, I thought that somehow a revelation would just hit me and I would be given the knowledge and advice I so desperately wanted. That never happened. Several months later, while watching the Daytona 500, I was overcome with the need to find a way to race - and I did. I found a way to race on a much lower budget – *my budget!* Because there were so few resources to turn to, this journey often led to learning the hard way and making many mistakes. Can an affordable wheel-to-wheel racing hobby be possible for the average Joe? Sure it can. I still can't help but wonder what a $1,500 weekend would be like. Hmm…a new set of the best tires for each race, a driving coach, a paid chef to prepare our meals (filet mignon and fine wine for the crew, of course), and a mechanic to work on the car between sessions. All right, maybe I am stretching things here, but you get the point. An exciting race weekend does not have to cost $1,500.

When looking at the costs of racing, one thing you need to keep in mind is that everyone will do things differently based on their resources and personal preferences. You need to do what is right for you. Is it necessary to have a race built engine and just about every go-fast part? Of course not. You might be surprised at how many people use stock engines. I used a stock engine for several years and was able to run mid-pack in a class with cars that had a higher performance potential than the class I race with now (with the same car). Do you need to only use the most expensive tires and change them after every race? No. Do you need a big rig or an expensive RV to bring your car to the track? No. You get the basic pattern here. But again, all of these answers depend on who you ask. As you will see in racing, there is a broad range in budgets. When it comes down to it, you are the one who chooses what budget fits your financial situation and goals. Especially in the beginning, I recommend that you focus on getting out on the track and gaining seat time. Wait until after you have gained some experience to worry about preparing your car more.

Throughout this book, there are many references to the Sports Car Club of America (SCCA) and National Auto Sports Association (NASA). I focus primarily on these two clubs due to their size and the fact that many other clubs use them as reference points. In fact, many smaller clubs even adopt their rules. To provide you some additional background, SCCA was founded in 1944 and as of 2008, has over 55,000 members. SCCA has the most active membership participation of any motorsports organization today with over 2,000 amateur and professional motorsports events each year. NASA was founded in 1991 and continues to grow at a steady pace and as of 2008, has approximately 10,500 members. While this book primarily references these two organizations, the same basic organizational model can be utilized for almost every other club.

It is important to note that, while this book will be an extremely helpful tool in your pursuit of obtaining your racing dreams, it is not a book promising miracles. It is unrealistic to go out and buy a prepared racecar and expect the purchase price to be the only cost associated with club racing other than entry fees. Unless you rent a racecar, you will need to maintain, store, and transport your vehicle, and replace parts that become damaged, broken, or worn out. I am sure you have many more questions, but at this point you need to take a deep breath and relax. This book will answer these questions and will discuss the typical costs of racing, from auto-crossing to high performance driving events, to club racing.

You may notice that there are many pictures (for people like me, who get bored easily), and several of the key points are highlighted to further help you. In order for the book content to flow, the masculine pronoun is utilized. Everyone will take a different path as they become involved in road racing, but this book will serve as a map to get you to your destination. It would be impossible for this book to be written for every individual's specific set of circumstances – financial, personal, racing background, etc. But this book will be a valuable guide to beginning a racing career no matter what budget or background you may have. It is inevitable that during your quest to begin racing you will run into some roadblocks. What is most important is how you approach and handle these obstacles. One can truly grow from the experiences.

To aid you in the budgeting process, the book includes many of the primary costs associated with racing as of 2008. These costs were obtained through various sources which are readily available to you and are median prices. If you take your time to compare prices, look for sales, and purchase used items, your cost may be less than what I have estimated in this book.

1.

The Club Racing Experience:
A Day at the Races

So, you're wondering what club racing is really like? It's hard to fully explain the feeling that you get from racing. Basically, it is like a portal into another world. No, not exactly like in a science fiction movie, but it does bring you to a place far away from the typical daily stresses you face. When at the track, you won't be thinking about work or things that need to get done at home. Don't get me wrong, racing does create a new set of stresses, but somehow race-related stress feels very different. Before I had ever participated in an event, I had envisioned what a race weekend would be like. I will admit it turned out to be different than what I had originally pictured, but for the better. People often ask, "How fast do you go when racing?" or "What are your ¼ mile times in that car?" Errr, about 110 mph and really, really slow. In all seriousness, it does not matter very much whether you drive 110 mph or 160 mph on a straightaway. The rush comes when you're pushing the car to its limit around a corner at 80 mph with another car mere inches from your driver's side door. It comes when you're going down the straight with another car right on your side and trying to out brake them going into a turn, wondering who will give in first. Who would ever guess how big of a thrill braking to the car's limit could be? Sounds a little strange, but it's true. A good analogy is when you drive down a highway at 70 mph; in itself it is pretty boring. Now imagine going 70 mph around some very twisty roads. Even at the same speed, it is a bit different isn't it? The same thing happens when driving on a track. The straights are typically a place where you can regain your composure and take a deep breath before you get to the twisty stuff again, even if you are going 160 mph.

Your Race Day Begins the Night Before

The night before the race, you decide to go to bed early and get a good night's sleep, primarily because you need to get up very early in the morning. You can't help but wonder if you forgot something and how things will go tomorrow in the race. All right, stop thinking about it! You have gone through the car and made sure everything is in working order. You even used a checklist to ensure that everything is packed. There can't be anything that you missed. Or is there? Did you pack the car's logbook? Hmm. Yeah, it is in the bag with the driver's suit. Do you have your novice permit? You tell yourself to stop worrying and begin to fall asleep but during the night you anxiously wake up. You begin to wonder what would happen if the alarm does not go off? Funny how on workdays that isn't a big concern. Finally, you are awoken by what is normally a horrible beeping sound, but not today! Today it is a beautiful, almost musical, monotonous, beeping. As you begin to get ready for the day you start feeling more anxious. As you drive toward the track the pit in your stomach begins to grow the closer you get. There it is, the entrance to the track. You hear the sounds of race engines and your heart begins to beat even faster. As you drive into the track's entrance you see some very impressive rigs and racecars. Now your mind begins to wonder if you are really ready. This is it.

When you arrive at the track, the first step is for you and your "crew" to go to registration. You walk up to registration prepared with a check (if you did not already prepay) and your racing license (or novice permit and log book). Your crew members are here with you, so they also register. The registration area is typically open for only a few hours in the morning – at least today you don't have to worry about making sure your crew gets there on time to sign-in. Now it's time to go down to the paddock and find a spot for your racecar and gear. When driving around, you are blown away by all of the expensive cars and equipment some people have! It is hard not to wonder how you will be able to compete against them.

After unpacking your car, it is time to go get your gear teched. At this point your racecar has already gone through the annual tech inspection (as outlined in chapter 5). You get to the tech "shed" with your helmet, the racecar's logbook, pen and a smile. The tech scrutinizers verify that you have an up-to-date logbook and that there are no outstanding issues with your racecar noted in the book. They also verify that your helmet meets the club's requirements. Not that you mind standing in line while you have a million other things to do, but you make a mental note to delegate this task to one of your "crew" next time. After the scrutinizer signs off on your log book for the event, you then put the sticker he gave you on the car to show you passed the tech inspection. This is nothing compared to the much more intensive annual tech inspection, but you know it is your responsibility to ensure that the car is in good working order.

Now you go through your car one more time and check the tire pressures, clean the windshield, re-torque the wheel lug nuts and check the engine oil level. "Where's my crew?" you exclaim. Oh, there they are having coffee, eating breakfast, and enjoying themselves while you prepare the car! Anyway, now you are ready to go. Today you are in race group six, so you will have some time before your qualifying session. You take a few moments to relax, but before you know it, it is time to go to the false grid. After several minutes of waiting on the grid it is your group's turn to go out on the track. You take a few more deep breaths just to help calm the nerves. Time to begin!

You have completed the qualifying session and obtained the results. Not bad at all. You qualified 12th out of 20 cars. Now for one of your favorite parts of the race day – taking some time to walk around, talk to fellow drivers and watch some of the other races. Before you even realize it, group five is starting to go out on the track. Ut-oh, you better get going! You say goodbye to everyone, and as you begin to walk to your car to change into your driver's suit, your nerves start up again. You drive over to the false grid and take your position. You look at the other cars on grid and begin your strategy for the start. Then you think, "Strategy? Shouldn't I have one?" At this point in your racing career there really is not much of a strategy other than remembering that you can't win a race on the first lap, but you can lose it. People have different approaches on how to handle the down time while on the false grid. Do you want to stay in the car and concentrate or do you want to get out of the car and talk to other drivers in your group? Shriek! Shriek!

"Five minutes! Five minutes!" the grid worker shouts. You get back into the car, put the window net up and tighten your belts. You close your eyes and visualize yourself driving a perfect lap around the track. "One minute! One minute!" the grid worker now shouts. At this point you can almost hear your heart beat. You raise your fist out the window indicating to the workers that your car is now running and ready to go. The grid worker points to the car that qualified on pole motioning for them to begin moving and the line begins to make its way out onto the track. Once you are in the proper grid position and have passed all of the workers that are out on the track itself, you start to warm-up the tires and brakes. You're careful not to get overzealous, as all too many people spin on the warm-up lap. How embarrassing! The field now begins to approach the starting line, and you can see the starter stare the field down. "Not yet, not yet," you think to yourself. It seems like this is taking forever! The field gets closer and closer. There it is, the green flag – go, go, go!

All of the emotions and activities during the day combined are what make club racing so much fun. There is much more to a racing event than just driving fast around a track that a prospective driver could easily overlook. Take a close look around the next time you attend a club racing event. You will see people helping their fellow competitors, laughing and, in general, having a great time. I always thought it was strange to see people assisting another competitor fix or prepare their racecar, but it happens all the time. The thing that really surprised me is that people who help you the most are often your fiercest competitors. I guess the easiest way to picture what it is like is to imagine a fraternity. And no, you won't be forced into running laps around the track in your underwear as an initiation, although that would be pretty funny! In racing, there will be times that on the spot car repairs will be necessary. It is just a fact when racing. When something does happen, you might be surprised at the amount of help you receive. At times it can even be a bit overwhelming, especially when you consider that the people helping may not even know you. To get a full appreciation you just have to experience it for yourself.

So, How Much Did That Day Just Cost You?

For you, the $250 - $350 entry fee just represents one of the associated costs. It gets a bit depressing when you really start figuring out what the event just cost. This time you were lucky because it does not appear that anything broke that would necessitate buying more replacement parts. You start adding the costs up in your head… There were tires, gas for the racecar and tow vehicle, brake pads were worn down a bit. Eeek! You begin to wonder how can racing costs be reduced?

For people like myself who simply can't afford to (or for others who simply don't want to) spend tons of money on racing, you become forced into finding ways to reduce the costs. Did you buy your gas at the track? During a time when 93 octane gas could be purchased for $3.80 at a gas station, it won't be unusual to see the track charge $7.50 or more per gallon for the same grade. Buy your gas at a local gas station and bring it with you. The one-time cost of a 5-gallon fuel jug (or maybe two) is well worth the investment. Do you send the racecar to a garage when it needs to be repaired? If you do, this adds up extremely fast. Learn how to work on the car yourself, and you will save a significant amount of money. Did you pay for a hotel? Why not camp at the track? I'll admit that I am a wimp and need a large tent, air mattress, and a fan. Just because you are camping does not mean that you can't do it with comfort. Take a close look at what you spend, and be creative with methods to cut your racing expenditures. More information about the costs associated with racing will be discussed throughout this book.

What Did it Cost the Club?

With entry fees ranging between $250 and $350, clubs must be making a significant amount of money from hosting events, right? At one of the recent SCCA two-day events, the entry fee was $280, which included a practice and qualifying session on Friday, then a race on Saturday. The event seemed to be on par with any other typical weekend for that track with 250 entrants. I whipped out my calculator and did some number crunching. For that one weekend alone, they took in $70,000 from entry fees. So why do they charge so much for the entry fee? I thought SCCA was supposed to be a non-profit club?

I spoke with a few clubs that host racing events regarding their costs. What I learned absolutely shocked me! The following information represents a portion of the costs for an SCCA region to host a two-day event in 2008, at the same track I referenced in the scenario above. While this track is a bit on the expensive side, it will give you an appreciation for where your entry fee goes.

- Track rental fee for a Friday / Saturday event: $46,000
- Insurance ($31 per entrant): $7,750
- Trophies: $1,000
- Water for volunteers (60 cases): $360
- Sanctioning fee: $350
- Food for worker appreciation party*: $4,000

- Beer for worker appreciation party (2 kegs)*: $950
- Costs for initial purchase and ongoing maintenance of equipment including fire extinguishers, radio communication systems, timing and scoring equipment, computers, tools, scales, flag sets, etc.

If you are like me, you are quickly adding up the above costs. The total for these listed expenses not including various equipment is $60,410. Again, these are just some of the expenses. There are many other smaller ticket items that add up quickly. (The costs will also vary depending upon the track and club.)

After reviewing these costs, you will notice that a figure for employees' salaries is not included, which for most businesses is very costly. Why is this? With SCCA and most other racing clubs, all flaggers, stewards, registration workers, and timing and scoring workers are all volunteers. To staff an event at SCCA's standards, it often takes nearly 100 volunteers for each race weekend. Yeah, that number seems high until you start adding all of the areas that volunteers are needed. For example, the club uses 3 or 4 workers per corner / flag station, 10 to 15 stewards, grid workers, fire and rescue workers, emergency medical staff, technical inspectors, pace car drivers, registration workers, and the list continues. Smaller clubs may not require this many volunteers, but still the number of people needed to host a successful event is not trivial. This is yet another reason why volunteers are so important to club racing's success. Can you imagine how much it would cost if all of these workers were paid?

* At the end of the day, SCCA normally hosts a worker appreciation party. Workers, drivers and their crew are all invited to attend for food, beer, and soda. It is a great time to meet the volunteers and swap racing stories with fellow drivers. Especially because people are volunteering their time, this is a small token of appreciation for the workers. Oh, the $4,000 budget for food and $950 for two kegs of beer are not misprints. When I was told the price for the two kegs of beer, I needed to ask several times "do you mean $95?" Here lies the problem. It is not possible for the club to bring their own food and drinks unless the party is done off the track premises. Since the parties are held on the track premises, food and drink must be purchased from the track, and are sold at consumer restaurant prices. Again, the club needs to keep their volunteers happy, therefore this party really is necessary. Without

volunteers, the event either wouldn't happen or the entrance fee would be substantially higher.

With many racing clubs, participants don't need to sign-up early and pay in advance. It is often possible for entrants to sign-up for an event and, on the day of the event, decide not to attend and receive their entry fee back. This equates to risk for the club. If it is a rainy day, the attendance is typically lower as compared to a nice, sunny day. The club uses historical data to estimate how many entries are anticipated, then calculates the necessary entry fee. What happens if the region is wrong? Hopefully they're not. Clubs do try to put some money aside from profitable events for a rainy day, no pun intended. It is also necessary for the club to budget for the competition licensing schools, where most clubs typically lose money. Think about the 60 students at a school and how much would be necessary to charge students to break-even. At the same time, without conducting licensing schools, no new drivers would be able to join the club.

As I previously mentioned, this pricing is only to provide you with an idea of what it costs clubs to host an event; each club, region, and track will have different costs. Often times smaller clubs have lower costs, but they also may have less desirable weekends or not as much staffing for the event.

It's More than Just Racing!

I have been to a few fairly significant events in terms of club racing. What I find interesting are the things I remember most fondly about the events. It is the camaraderie between racers, family and friends. Going into these events, I thought my memories would revolve around the driving aspect, but I was wrong. Believe me, I am totally into driving cars at the edge and becoming the best driver I can be, but you can't underestimate the other aspects of racing. Each race my wife Melissa and I attend, the more great people we meet. Through racing, I have developed several close friendships. The time you spend off the track is just as important and rewarding as the time spent on the track. Let's just say that racing is much more than I ever anticipated there would be.

2.

Getting Your Feet Wet

I fully understand that the idea of starting to race can be intimidating. I was in the same position not so long ago myself. There are many common questions and concerns people have. How can I start racing? Will I be able to afford it? What happens if I finish last? My car is not nearly as prepared as many others, so how will I ever be able to compete with them? What if this? What if that? One of my friends told me a story that really helped put things into perspective. While at a race as a spectator, he talked to his wife about how badly he felt for one of the drivers. "That driver is so far behind everyone else that is racing. That must be really awful." I know when I watched races in the past, I used to think the same exact thing – "That poor person!" Of course, it often takes the wisdom of a woman to set us men straight. "Who should feel bad for whom? *You* are the one sitting here on the hill and not driving. I feel sorry for *you*, not him!" She was absolutely right. Keep in mind that running in the back of the pack is the worst-case scenario. But when you really think about it, that worst-case scenario really is not so bad. And by all means, I am not saying that you will be running in the back of the pack.

This may sound obvious, but one of the first things you need to do is determine where road course racetracks are located in your area. Once you have identified the tracks in your general area, start looking at the tracks' schedules and identify clubs that race or hold high performance driving events (HPDE) there. The majority of tracks list the upcoming schedule on their websites, as well as the clubs that the track hosts events for. The appendix of this book includes a few good web sites for you to use. Many of these sites provide a huge wealth of knowledge, not only about the tracks in the area, but on many, many other topics as well.

At this beginning stage, you may or may not already have some money put aside to begin racing. Even if you have no money available right now, it certainly does not mean you should wait to get started. I am not saying to charge everything on a credit card or anything silly like that, but there are many different ways to begin the process. In fact, even if you do have the money to race right now, it is still important to attend a few races and get a feel for club racing and the specific club(s) your are thinking of racing with. Each racing club and region has its differences. While at the events, don't be afraid to walk around the paddock and ask lots of questions. People just love to talk about their racecars and share stories. Try to stay away from talking to people about costs associated with racing, as it will most likely be discouraging. Remember that a part of the reason you are reading this book is to learn how to race at a moderate cost, so don't focus too much of your time on this aspect while at the races. Instead, try to get a feel for the club and how it operates.

There are several organizations that hold club racing events. Two of the biggest organizations in the United States are the Sports Car Club of America (SCCA) and National Auto Sport Association (NASA). In addition to SCCA and NASA, there are many other smaller clubs that are also worth looking into. So if one of the clubs is not what you expected or hoped it would be, don't give up. Try attending another club's event to see if that is a better match for you. You might wonder how clubs can be different from one another. As an example, one club I race with has racecars that are prepared at many differing levels. At this club's events, it is not uncommon to see people who have spent a significant amount of money on their cars and equipment. Other clubs are much more laid back, and as a general rule, the cars are not prepared to the extent of the previously-referred-to club. Especially as a new person to the sport, this can be nice because you can be much more competitive on a smaller budget. Various clubs may also attract different crowds to their events. Although the two clubs I race with are unique in their own way, they complement each other nicely.

As you begin to get a better idea of which club you are interested in racing with, it will be worthwhile to get a copy of the club's rulebook. The majority of the rulebooks can be found on the clubs' website. Some of these rulebooks can be quite lengthy, but don't be overwhelmed by their size. When I first saw the SCCA rulebook and started flipping through the pages, I kept thinking, "How in the world will I be able to learn all of this?" Now that I have gained familiarity with how it is put together, it really is not as bad as it had appeared. Keep in mind that these rulebooks are written to cover several types of club racing classes.

The rulebook will soon become your bible of racing. While providing you the ultimate wisdom, it also can be confusing as heck and cause you to swear once or twice at the rule gods. When in doubt if something is legal or not, seek guidance from this holy book, and be sure to live to the letter of the rulebook. There is wrath and many headaches for those who don't follow the word of the book.

Creating a Plan

Have you developed a plan and established what your racing goals and expectations are? If not, now is the perfect time to do it. What do you want to accomplish in racing? What type of car do you want to race? Do you "need" to win races? Maybe you will begin racing a car that is only capable of running mid-pack during the first few years. After gaining experience, you may plan to purchase another car capable of being a front-runner, or work on further preparing the car you have been racing to its full potential. Perhaps you are like many people who race and are happy to be out there racing and don't need to win or be at the front of the pack. This does not mean that in time you can't work your way to the front of the pack. Believe me, whether you are battling for 16th place or 1st place, you will have a blast. A good initial goal is to focus on simply getting out on the track and then worry about winning later on in your career. As with establishing any set of goals, you should establish some short-term goals, as well as long-term goals. When setting these goals, keep them reasonable, and don't place unrealistic expectations on yourself. A goal such as beating Michael Schumacher in a Formula One race after your first year does not exactly seem realistic. Also, remember that you can always revisit your goals and adjust them. If you really want to win, you need to be aware of what it takes: lots of money, time, testing, money, frustration, time, and money. The Moving On chapter discusses what it takes to become a front-runner in further detail, but for now, let's focus on getting out on the track and not worry about winning just yet.

Time to Volunteer

A great way to learn more about racing is to volunteer for the club that you want to race with. Almost all clubs would absolutely love to have you volunteer in one capacity or another. But, of course, what you really want to know is how this is going to help you. First and foremost, it can be an enjoyable experience. There are many people who simply decide that volunteering is their thing and don't race at all. Volunteering can also be a great way to get your friends and family involved. I certainly have gained a true appreciation for volunteers' efforts and the work they do. Without volunteers, many clubs wouldn't exist. Until you have volunteered yourself, you won't truly understand what it is like. Another significant benefit is that you will meet many great people who are very knowledgeable about racing and who know the right people. These connections you make through volunteering will pay off later in your racing career. You might even hear of someone who is selling his racecar at a modest price through this experience. You know the old saying, "It is not what you know, but who you know." You better believe this also applies to racing as well.

One area that I highly recommend you volunteer for, from a future racer's perspective, is flagging. Flagging will provide you the closest seat in the house to the racing action. Many flaggers have volunteered for several years, and from this experience they often have gained the understanding of the fastest line through the turns and know what to be on the look-out for. If you have a choice of flagging stations, and if you have driven the track before, try to pick the stations that you find most difficult to drive. If you have never driven the track, think about the key turns on the track and start there. No matter what station you flag at, it is still going to be a great learning experience. And again, getting to know the people who may be flagging while you are out on the track never hurts.

There are also many other areas you can become involved with, depending upon your interests. It certainly is not a bad idea to try volunteering in a couple of different areas. A few other areas for which you can volunteer include registration (where all racers, crew, and workers must go to check in for a race), tech inspection (where racers' gear and cars are verified to be safe), and the timing / scoring booth. Some of these areas may seem a bit daunting at first, but any decent club will have people to coach you through the process. Since the focus of this book is to help you reach the goal of racing yourself, I won't discuss the other various areas for which you can volunteer. Just know that if you or someone else you know is interested in volunteering, there are many possible areas in which clubs would welcome assistance.

The other way you can volunteer is to offer your assistance to a racer and become a part of their "pit crew." There is a lot to learn about getting started in racing, and it can be helpful to crew for an experienced racer. Unfortunately, it is not as glamorous as the NASCAR pit crews jumping over walls and changing tires during a race. In fact, other than endurance racing, there are no pit stops (at least not intended ones). Depending on whom you crew for, you might only be doing simple things such as cleaning the windshield, checking the oil level, and adjusting the tires pressure. Well, that is until something unexpected happens. These unexpected happenings are often great learning experiences. By crewing for another racer, you will gain from all of the experience that the person has, as well as from other racers that pit around him or her. You do want to make sure that you crew for someone who knows what he is doing. That is not to say they have to be a master mechanic or always tuning their car, but he should be a decent driver, respectful to their fellow competitors, and understand the basic rules of the club he is racing with. There is not much helpful information to be learned from someone who has bad habits or a total lack of racing knowledge. You should also try to crew for someone who has a similar car, or who races in a similar class as you would like to. For example, if you plan on racing in Improved Touring with

SCCA, it still might be fun to crew for someone who races an open wheel racecar, but it won't be nearly as valuable as crewing for another Improved Touring driver. While crewing, don't be afraid to ask questions, especially during the down times. The person you are crewing for expects you to ask questions. Helping you learn and acting as a mentor is often why people have crew members. At the club racing level, most people really could care less if they have to wash their own windows themselves or not. Racers enjoy passing along their knowledge and helping new people become involved in racing. People realize that you are crewing to gain experience and have a fun time. After all, that is what club racing is all about. In time you will have the opportunity to return the favor to someone else.

When I was trying to get into racing, many people stated that I really should crew for someone for at least a year or two before racing myself. While crewing for someone else can be a good learning experience, I don't agree that it is necessary. If you have the means to race now or in the near future, do it. One thing you will learn about club racing is that you are never alone. Fellow racers are almost always willing to lend a helping hand, even if you have never met them before.

Autocross – Racing with Very Little Investment

As previously said, one year as I was watching the Daytona 500, the need to race seemed to hit me all at once. I just had to find a way to become involved in racing. But how? I had very little money, which did not exactly help matters. I am not talking about low-budget-racing, but much closer to no-budget-racing. Regardless, that day I became determined to do something to get me closer to my racing dreams. You just have to love the internet! While on-line, I stumbled across information about autocrossing. If you are not familiar with autocross events (also known as Solo II), they are events where you can take your ordinary streetcar as-is, and race it in a very safe and controlled environment. When I say "very safe," I mean in an empty parking lot where the worst thing you could hit is an orange cone. And no, it is not wheel-to-wheel racing, so you won't have to worry about hitting another car. Each driver competes against other drivers in their respective class by taking a timed lap around a temporary course defined by traffic cones one car at a time. Of course, the goal is to drive the course as fast as you can. Ah, but you don't have a sports car. No problem! You can race almost any type of car, regardless if it has an automatic or manual transmission. You will see everything from ordinary Honda Civics and station wagons to race-prepared cars. Due to potential rollover issues, sport utility vehicles are almost never allowed.

Let me ask you, have you ever wished that there were no speed limits or safety concerns to worry about while driving on an open, curvy road? Here is your chance to do it legally, and actually be encouraged to go faster. How cool is that? If you are picturing a cheesy course with someone timing you with a stopwatch, think again. In fact, most clubs have very sophisticated (and expensive) timing systems that calculate the lap time to a thousandth of a second. To make things a bit more challenging, you can't just barrel through the course, knocking over cone after cone in an attempt to get a fast time. Each cone hit has a time penalty associated with it, which is typically two seconds. Knocking just one cone over will usually ruin that run's time. Speeds on autocross courses typically peek in the 40 – 50 mph range and contain many turns to test your skills. These speeds may sound slow, but when you are out there yourself, that feeling will certainly change. It is much harder then you might think.

Initially, the course may simply look like a sea of cones out there. But after walking the course a few times, it will begin to make more sense. The first couple of times you drive an autocross, it seems that half of the game is to figure out where you should be going. As with almost anything else in life, after doing it a few times, it becomes much easier. I would recommend that you ask for an instructor to ride with you for the first few runs, until you get the feel for it. The instructor won't only guide you through the course, but hopefully will provide suggestions on how to approach various sections.

One of the keys to any form of racing, especially in the beginning, is getting seat time. Focus on seat time and not the go-fast parts! It is much cheaper and more effective to spend your money on participating in more events.

In addition to the driving aspect, autocrossing is also a very social event. That said, one of the things that I have a hard time getting used to is the amount of time there is between runs. With the clubs that I have autocrossed with, there could be 45 minutes in between each run. Take this time to talk to more-experienced racers and learn as much as you can.

Not only are autocross events an extremely safe place to push you car hard, but it also provides valuable learning tools that apply to your daily driving. What are some of the things you will learn? How to control the car at its limit, thresh-hold-braking (braking to the maximum potential of your car's braking system), and the importance of looking ahead. So if a deer jumps out in front of your car (or worse yet, a child), you will already have the built-in reflexes to react to the situation and the experience to control the car at the limit. In all seriousness (although it is a pretty good excuse to participate in the events), what you learn here could save your life as well as others. And yes, cone marks do easily come off your car if you happen to kill a few during an autocross event. The car control techniques you learn autocrossing will also be helpful to you when driving out on a racetrack.

An autocross entry fee is usually between $20 and $30 per driver. During the day you will get four or more attempts to get the best timed run possible. (A typical lap around the course is between 40 – 60 seconds.) After the timed runs, many clubs have "fun runs" for an additional cost of $1 or $2 per run. A fun run is exactly what it sounds like. You go out there and just have fun and the times don't count towards the competition. I always look forward to this part of the event. Usually with fun runs you can have a passenger ride along in your car with you, as long as they are also participating in the event. Now is your chance to give your friends a thrill and show them what you can do.

Preparation Before the Autocross Event

How do you determine where autocross events are held in your area? Do what I did, and take advantage of the internet. Simple internet searches of autocross and Solo II driving events, followed by the state you live in, will provide a good start. You can also use some of the internet chat forums listed in the back of this book to find information and clubs that hold autocross events in your area. Before going to the event, be sure to determine if the club has any unique rules that you need to be aware of. For participants who are under 18 years old, check to see if they need a minor waiver form signed by a parent or guardian.

So what do you need to do to prepare your car for an autocross? This is the nice thing – very little. Make sure that your brakes are working well and the car is in decent overall shape by doing things like checking the oil and coolant levels. Basically, these are the types of things you should be doing routinely even if you are not autocrossing. (Yeah, I know, not all of us check these things nearly as often as we should.) You also need to make sure that the battery is secure and does not move around easily. If it does, go to your local automotive parts store and purchase a battery tie down bracket (approximately $10). You also need to clean out the car. I am sure we all have friends (or maybe you are guilty of this) who seem to bring their whole life with them in their car. It always cracks me up to watch one of my friends get to an event and start unloading his car. I look over and see a large pile of stuff on the ground next to his car. If you are one of these people, do yourself a favor and keep most of this stuff home.

One important thing you will need is a driving helmet. Fortunately, most clubs have loaner helmets; you should check with them prior to the event to determine if they do or not. If you have the ability to borrow a motorcycle or automotive helmet from someone you know, all the better. If you decide that you would rather purchase your own, a new motorcycle helmet can be purchased for about $180. While a motorcycle helmet can be used for autocrossing and high performance driving events, it won't be allowed for competitive wheel-to-wheel racing, which requires the helmet to have an automotive rating.

White shoe polish will also be helpful. Not black, but white. I went to my local grocery store and found it there; many other places carry white shoe polish as well. Maybe you will be able to borrow someone else's white shoe polish while at the event. You may be wondering what in the world is up with white shoe polish? I know it sounds strange, but I will explain this to you soon.

On the morning of the event you will most likely have to increase your tires' air pressure. If it is not necessary, then you are probably running your pressures too high for day-to-day use. Why increase your tire pressures? The reason is to keep your tires from rolling onto the sidewalls during the severe cornering that the car will do during the event. If your tires roll over, you can cause damage to the tire, and you also will not get the most traction possible. Many factors go into determining the optimum tire pressure, such as how heavy your car is, the weight distribution, tire type, your personal preference, and the weather conditions. A good starting point is the maximum recommended tire pressure as stated on the sidewall of the tire. If you have low-profile performance tires, you may be able to start at a slightly lower pressure. While this serves as an approximate starting tire pressure, what is most important is the tire pressure right after the run. If you plan to go to a gas station for air on the way to the event, I would suggest leaving a bit early, just in case. I remember one event which a few friends and I attended. When we got to the gas station where we typically get air, it was out of service. No problem, right? There is another gas station on the way. When we got to that gas station, we found out that they did not have air. After some more looking around, we ended up going to the event to register and then had to leave again on a mission to find air for our tires. Needless to say, it was a real pain in the butt! You should also have a decent tire pressure gauge to measure and make adjustments while at the event. It is not necessary to buy a very expensive gauge, but it should be something better then the $1.50 convenience store air gauge. Refer to the Basic Recommended Tools section in the Repairs and Maintenance chapter for information on air gauges. Oh, and while you are at the gas station, don't fill the car up all the way with gas. You should try to arrive at the track with between a ¼ - ½ tank of gas, depending on how far away the gas station is to the event. The purpose of this is to keep the weight of the car as low as possible and thus increase the power to weight ratio. Of course, keep in mind that you do also need to get back home or to the gas station after the event. Believe it or not, I have seen people not able to make it to a gas station after an event. If you have a full tank of gas, don't worry about it. If you are 0.1 second slower in the beginning, it really does not matter as you should first be focusing on learning as much as possible.

At the Autocross Event

On the day of the event, arrive early to register and get ready for the day. If you live in a northern climate, it seems that especially in the beginning of the year, after everyone has been going through winter racing withdrawal, events are extremely well-attended. It won't be much fun if you got to the event just to find out that it is sold out. While registering, ask if there is a novice class and if there are instructors available to help novices. Clubs typically have a novice class and "course walks" to explain the basic techniques. It may also be possible to have an instructor ride with you until you feel comfortable. I would highly recommend taking advantage of this. As a part of the registration, you will be asked basic information about the car you will be driving, such as the year, make, model and what modifications you may have done to it. This information will determine in which class your car is placed. Cars entered in the event will be put into different classes based upon the vehicles' performance potential. So no matter if you have a Porsche 911 twin turbo or a very old Honda Prelude, you will be competing against similar cars.

For novices, many clubs utilize a PAX index system which handicaps vehicles to allow a comparison of lap times for cars that are not in the same class. The index is built upon a large national database of SCCA autocross results. The goal of the PAX index is to take the driver out of the equation and compare only the car's performance potential. Your vehicle's PAX index is multiplied against your run time to provide you the PAX time. By using this PAX index, you are able to compare your times against other people who are driving cars that would normally be in other car classes. It is a nice way for you to compete against other novice drivers.

While at the event, don't be afraid to ask for help. Most experienced autocrossers enjoy helping others, especially people new to the sport. When registering, ask about the work assignments. Yes, typically each entrant has to work a little during the event. The "work" simply involves being at one of the corner stations and calling in car numbers that knock down cones, as well as putting them back in their marked box. The amount of time that you have to work varies from club to club, but on average you will work one or two ½ hour shifts during the day. Ask if you can work as early in the day as possible so you can watch other drivers and how they approach the course. After registering, begin to prepare your car for the tech inspection. For the most part, each club will check for the same basic things to ensure you have a safe day. Some of the common things tech inspectors look at are as follows:

- Check to make sure that your helmet meets the club's requirements.
- Verify that all loose items are removed from the car (usually includes floor mats). Can you imagine how distracting it would be to have stuff flying around the interior while out on the course?
- Inspect your wheels and tires to verify that they are in decent shape. If someone pulls on the tire and it wobbles due to bad bearings or whatever, it is not exactly safe.
- Verify that the engine compartment has no major leaks and that the battery is secure.
- Car numbers and class must be visible. Since clubs typically don't provide you numbers, this is one place where the white shoe polish is very handy. Check the registration packet to determine what number you are assigned. Use the shoe polish to make your numbers on the rear side windows. The shoe polish will easily come off your glass windows with a standard window cleaning solution. Don't be silly by putting it on the paint of your car! It will be very difficult to remove and may damage the vehicle's paint. Another alternative to using shoe polish is to use painter's tape.

You may also want to take out your spare tire while at the event, although it is usually not a requirement to pass the technical inspection. There is no reason to lug around that extra weight when it is so easy to take out. After having your car teched, it is time to walk the course a few times. If there is a novice walk through, I highly recommend that you participate it. During the novice walk, an instructor will give some advice on the recommended driving lines, where to brake, and other overall driving techniques to be applied to the course. If you have time before the novice walk through, you should walk the course a few times. While walking it, visualize where you should be driving the course and actually walk that line. It is also helpful to crouch down a bit in various areas to get to the approximate height you will be looking at the course from the driver's seat. While walking the course, focus on looking ahead. If you can't see two or three gates ahead, there is a good chance you will get lost when you drive it in your car. If you just go and simply walk it just for the sake of doing so, the only thing you will gain is some exercise. Before doing your first run, you should use the handy-dandy shoe polish again. This time you will be putting a small line on the tires from the tread down the tire a little, as shown in the pictures. What you are doing here is using the shoe polish to provide feedback on your tire pressures. In the beginning, you most likely won't be using the tire to its full potential. At this point your primary objective is to make sure that you don't need to add air to the tire. After a few runs, when you have increased your speeds a bit, you should look at the shoe polish line a bit closer and adjust the tire pressures accordingly.

(Pressure too low)   (Correct pressure)   (Pressure too high)

If pressures are correct, the line of shoe polish will be worn off right around the end of the tread and just before the sidewall. Many tire manufactures put an arrow on the tire to indicate where the tire should optimally contact pavement under cornering. If the line is not apparent past the tread and a little way down the tire sidewall, you need to add more air before your next run. If there is shoe polish on the tread still, you should decrease the tire pressure a little bit. Before making any tire pressure adjustments, write down the starting and ending pressures for the next time you do an autocross event. At least this way you will have a reference point to begin with. Oh, and don't forget to lower your tire pressures after the event if you raised them beyond the normal recommended pressure indicated on your vehicle's door jam.

At the end of the day you will be able to find out who won the various classes, and possibly even win a trophy yourself. The main goal is to have fun and hopefully learn a thing or two about car control. No matter what the event's result sheet states, don't be disappointed. It can take a lot of experience to become a fast driver. Again, just concentrate on learning as much as you can.

A few basic things to bring to the autocross event:

- Your driver's license
- Money for the entrance fee and fun runs
- A helmet that meets the clubs requirements
- Water, and lots of it
- Lunch
- Sunscreen
- Sunglasses
- Hat / cap
- Folding chair
- Tire pressure gauge
- White shoe polish
- Paper and a pen
- Bug spray

As you will learn, autocrosses can range from simply a day and a time to hang out with friends to running national events that are very, very competitive. The amounts of money people spend preparing their cars also ranges significantly. At most events, you will see some very well-prepared cars that use special autocross tires (the tires have a softer rubber compound that heats up very quickly, and really sticks to the pavement) to people simply using their ordinary daily commuter street tires.

I know first-hand that it can be extremely tempting to go out and buy some of these go-fast parts, but don't spend money your money now! Do a few more autocross events with your car as-is and get as much seat time as possible..

If you really want to do something to upgrade your car, go out and buy some better street tires after the ones you currently have on your car are worn out. If you intend to participate in high performance driving events in the near future, consider buying an inexpensive extra set of rims for these tires. The best thing you can do to decrease your lap times is to focus on learning as much as you possibly can about race driving techniques. There are some very good racing books and web sites that focus on this subject (a few of which are listed in the back of this book). Buying books like these is money well spent.

Summary of Primary Costs:

Autocrossing is a great way for the beginner or experienced driver to learn how to make more speed, develop car control, and learn many of the mental aspects of racing. Best of all, it is pretty darn cheap.

- Entry fee: The average entry fee is between $20 and $30. Typically after the timed runs, clubs have fun runs that cost an additional $1 to $2 per run.
- Tire wear: It is a bit difficult to provide you a figure for tire wear. A lot depends on how you drive the car, the tires you have on the vehicle, etc. Of course you will see a decrease in tire life, but overall autocrossing is not very hard on tires.
- Helmet: If possible, borrow one from the club or someone you know. If you decide to purchase a helmet, a motorcycle helmet can be purchased for about $180.

Time to Drive on a Racetrack: High Performance Driving Events

As previously mentioned, I had always thought that it would be necessary to spend a small fortune to actually get out on a racetrack. As I continued to watch club races at my local track (Lime Rock Park in Connecticut), I heard people talking about going out on the track with their cars in some type of driving event. For some reason I assumed they were only talking about using high-priced sports cars such as Corvettes, Porsches, and Ferraris, but I was mistaken. What I heard intrigued me to learn more about these high performance driving events (HPDEs). Oh, just to keep you on your toes, some clubs call these events by other names such as "Performance Driving Experience" (PDX) or "Performance Driving Event" (PDE). I learned that people can use regular streetcars; it does not have to be a high performance sports car. I know what you may be thinking. There is no way that you would take your streetcar, on which you rely on a daily basis, out on the track. You simply can't risk damaging the car that is your only means of transportation. You may also be thinking that your car is simply too slow to bring out there and might prove to be quite embarrassing. I experienced both of these feelings at different times. At first I brought "my baby," a 1996 Mitsubishi 3000GT, a car that I had wanted for many years. When I thought about bringing the car to the track, I was not worried about the car being too slow, but I was very concerned about damaging it. My first event was a bit stressful because I was so nervous about getting any chips and scratches on the car, or crashing it for that matter. The goal at this point in your career should be to simply make it through the event without damaging the car, or even worse, hurting yourself. Use this as an opportunity to learn if you are interested in pursuing racing further, and of course, having fun. What I realized from this experience was that I was interested in doing more driving events, and that I wanted to further pursue wheel-to-wheel road racing.

While there are risks associated with participating in HPDEs, it is not nearly as dangerous as some may think. All HPDE clubs that I am aware of have a special run group for novices. In the novice run group, each driver has an instructor ride with him while out on the track to provide guidance and to make sure that everyone is driving safely and within their capabilities. If you are using a racecar in these events, be aware that the instructor typically needs the same harness system (seat belts) that the driver has. While out on the track, you can't simply pass cars any place on the track, the turns, in particular. There are designated passing zones, which are limited to straight-aways; often clubs require the driver being passed to point you by. The first several times out on the track, you will probably find it can be a bit tough to get used to everything that is going on all at once. That is one reason why you have an instructor to act as your second set of eyes and to watch for any potential issues. This is not to say that you shouldn't be as alert as possible. Pay special attention to the flaggers giving you vital information. You will be on the track with other novices in a separate group from other experienced drivers, so there is no pressure to go fast, and you will have time to get accustomed to all of the details on which you need to concentrate. Focus on learning the proper driving lines and being safe. There are no rewards, nor driving scouts out there looking for the next Michael Andretti.

Driving on a track was much different than I had anticipated. When I had previously watched some of the races, it had looked like they were not going very fast. I had always thought that I was a very good driver, and that I would also be really fast out on the track. Needless to say, it was much more difficult than I had thought it was going to be. I remember my instructor telling me, "Remember to look at the corner worker stations, and check your mirrors often." I thought, "Yeah right, take my eyes off where I am going and look in the mirrors?" I also found that I was not able to look at the flagging stations as much as I should have. As the day progressed, my comfort and confidence levels continued to grow. I thought it was really funny that while I was at the event, I was enjoying myself, but I had not caught the racing bug…at least not yet. I am sure it was because I felt a bit stressed with everything going on. Looking back on it the next day, my perspective really changed. I guess things just needed to settle in, and I got over the initial stress of doing my first event. The following day, all I could think about was how badly I wanted to do another event as soon as possible!

Did I tell you that in the second run session of my first HPDE I spun the car? I was going through a turn and felt the car sliding. So I did exactly what I shouldn't have and suddenly lifted off the gas. It felt like the spin lasted a few minutes and everything really slowed down. What a helpless feeling! There was no damage to the car, but it hurt my confidence level. I spoke with an instructor about what had happened and decided to go back out on the track. After the next session, I was able to build my confidence level back up a bit. At the same time this made me begin to seriously think about what other options there were, instead of using the 3000GT. My wife recommended that I use our old 1987 Honda Prelude si that we kept for winter driving. Yes, I loved the 3000GT so much that we used the Prelude that was in "a bit rough shape," and had a ton of miles on it. All right, maybe saying a bit rough shape is being very kind and a ton of miles meant over 170,000 miles on the stock suspension and engine. And the paint? Yeah, that wasn't very pretty either. I remember the time I started the Prelude up in my garage and my neighbor came running over because he thought our house was on fire. So, it smoked a little when I first started it. That was really embarrassing, but pretty funny now when I look back at it. When my wife first mentioned the idea of using the Honda, I thought she was crazy. I could just picture it: I park next to a Porsche 911 start the car, and tons of smoke comes out of the exhaust! After a bit more of her convincing and my thinking about it, I decided to try it and performed some basic maintenance in order to get it ready for the track. I was also a little intimidated about driving a car with only 110 horsepower with the other high horsepower cars that would be on the track with me.

In addition to having an instructor in your car when you are driving, there are often classroom sessions to discuss driving technique. During the first classroom session, I asked if there were any unique lines for lower horsepower cars versus higher horsepower cars. The instructor asked me more about my car and how much horsepower I was talking about. When I said 110, several people chuckled, and I felt a bit embarrassed. In the next session out on the track, not only was I keeping up with the other higher horsepower cars, I was actually passing them. Now that was a huge rush! After the session, I remember one guy who was driving one of those exotic cars come over to check out my car ask me what modifications I did to it. My reply was, "One of those air intake things, but that's it." He just looked at the car in shock. He then asked, "Did you modify the engine?" I just smiled and said no. I, too, was in shock to see him looking at my old, junky car. How weird was that? A guy driving an amazing Ferrari came to check out my old, junky Prelude? And yes, he was one of the people I passed while out on the track! You may be wondering how a car could pass another car that has much higher horsepower on a straight – the answer is corner exit speed. In my case, I was taking the turn preceding the straight at 90 mph while the other car was only taking it at 70 mph. Even with all of the extra horsepower, the other car could not compensate for the much higher exit speed. This was when I truly learned just how much the driver impacts things, and that you don't need an expensive or high horsepower car to have a great time out on the track! It is important to realize that the car is only one part of the equation. I also learned that people who bring less expensive cars are not as worried about damaging their vehicles and often learn faster than people who are afraid of hurting their car and thus tend to hold back much more. (This certainly is not to say that driving a high horsepower car wouldn't be a blast to drive on the track.)

After taking the Prelude out on the track, I gained a new respect and liking for the car. Before I never really cared about the Prelude or gave much thought to fixing it up. But now it was no longer our junky, old winter car. In my head, it became my racecar! I began to work on the car and made it more presentable – I fixed the oil leaks, patched some of the rust holes with Bondo, and eventually painted it myself. This was the beginning of the end.

Is there a requirement to participate in HPDEs before entering a club racing school? Although it is not a requirement, I honestly wish it were. This comes from both a new racer's perspective, as well as from a person who has racing experience. I am not saying that a person needs to spend years doing HPDEs, but one should at least do a few events before moving on to wheel-to-wheel racing. Do yourself a favor and participate in HPDEs until you feel comfortable being out on the track. (I can't even imagine having one of my first track experiences being a full out SCCA or NASA race school.) While these schools briefly touch upon the proper and fastest racing lines, it is much easier to learn it at your own pace without having to worry about cars passing you anywhere and everywhere on the track. When you first go out on a track, there are many, many things on which you need to concentrate. First and foremost, you need to drive safely and be aware of your surroundings. In a HPDE, you have time to build up your speed at your own pace and concentrate on learning the proper racing lines. You will also have an instructor ride in the car along with you until you and he feels confident that you are ready to go out on your own. This is not the case when you participate in a club's race school. When you enter a race school to get your license, you had better already have this basic knowledge, or things will be extremely difficult for you. In the racing schools, the club will often have instructors out on the track driving their own racecars to see how you react to them doing various things, such as getting very close to you and staying there, passing you, and letting you pass them. The room for error when wheel-to-wheel racing is much, much less than in a HPDE. Yes, I have seen people who jump right into racing without going to HPDEs or another comprehensive type of race school. What often happens is that they are not as safe on the track in a race situation as they should be. These drivers often become the drivers everyone says to watch out for. By going out and participating in one of the race schools to get a race license without any previous track time, you are jeopardizing your safety as well as that of your fellow drivers. "Wheel-to-wheel racing" is not just a saying.

You will be racing with cars that are less than a few feet (and many times just inches) from your car through the turns with both of you pushing the cars to the limits. Additionally, a person without enough track experience won't have as much fun as a person who is comfortable out on the track. Keep in mind that, while racing, you won't just be out on the track with other novices. Instead, you will be out there with some very experienced drivers who will be passing you just about anywhere. I am not trying to scare you about the race schools or racing in general; once you have gotten some seat time, you will be ready for it. The point of this is to make sure that you are safe and that you enjoy your experience. The Going Back to School chapter will give you a better idea of what a typical club's race school for licensing is really like.

You may also be wondering what experience you need before doing a HPDE. There is no necessary formal training you need before doing a high performance driving event. It can be useful to do some auto-cross events to become better at controlling your car, but it is not a prerequisite.

Preparation Before the High Performance Driving Event

- Brake Pads and rotors: One of the most important things when driving on a track is to have a good working brake system. Can you imagine going 100 mph on a straight only to get to a turn and find out that the brakes are not working properly? So the number one task is to check your brake pads and rotors. What type of brake pads do you need? Unless you are driving a high performance sports car, a Corvette for example, which already uses a very high performance brake pad, I would suggest you purchase a set of high performance brake pads for the front of the car. (Even in racing conditions, I often use stock rear pads with my front wheel drive car.)

- Change your brake fluid if it has not been done recently. Flushing your brakes with a high quality brake fluid is very important and needs to be done at least once a year, especially when driving the car on a track. Changing your brake fluid is much easier to do yourself (with an assistant) than it may sound. Worst case, bring it to a garage and have them do it. Don't underestimate the importance of doing this, or you may just find out the hard way.
- Verify that your wheels and tires are in decent shape.
- Do a suspension check. Jack up one side of the car at a time and pull on the wheel on the top and sides. There should be very little play, or as some may say, it shouldn't "wobble." This will help ensure that the car's ball joints, wheel bearings, and tie rods are in decent shape.
- Make sure the engine does not have any major leaks from oil or antifreeze. I am not talking about an occasional drip here and there.
- If you have not changed your oil recently (within the past two months), it would be worthwhile to change it to help preserve your engine. You also need to make sure you have enough oil in your car so the engine does not starve for oil when going around the turns. But make sure you don't over-fill it.
- Verify that the battery is secured. If it does not have a battery tie down bracket, go out to your local auto parts store and purchase one. These are usually sold for less then $10.00.
- Verify that the brake lights work.
- Helmet: Be sure to check the club's helmet requirements. Do they accept motorcycle (M) helmets or do they require the helmet to be certified for automobiles (SA)? Also, assuming the club requires that the helmet has a Snell rating, what is the oldest year certification they will accept? Although some clubs may allow you to borrow a helmet, I suggest you get

your own. It will be one less thing you need to worry about once at the event. Helmets are discussed in greater detail in the "How Safe is Club Racing?" chapter.

- Do you need a membership in the club? Some clubs that host HPDEs require that you become a member of their club before you can participate in their events.
- Determine if there are any club specific requirements. For example, all clubs I have participated with require entrants to wear long pants. (Yes, even during the hot summer months!) Some also have a requirement for entrants to wear long sleeve shirts made out of cotton.
- Does your car meet the club's requirements? For example, it is usually required for convertible cars to have a roll bar.
- It would be a good idea to purchase a standard 5-gallon fuel jug. Most tracks have fuel pumps open for a specified period of time during the event, but it makes things much easier if you don't have to worry about this. As an instructor, I always hear students panicking about what specific times the pumps are open. Bringing your own gas will also save you some money. If you use a fuel jug, it is highly recommended that you buy the gas as close to the track as possible to avoid transporting it very far in your vehicle. Transporting fuel can be hazardous.

People commonly ask about the type of tires that should be used. Unless you have a high performance sports car such as a Corvette, which already has very high performance tires, you should consider getting a set of rims and tires to use for HPDEs at some point. Why? Many tires are not capable of standing up to the beating they receive at the track and will get destroyed. Take a look at what happened when I tried using my standard street tires. The tire was not able to withstand the heat generated by driving on the track, which caused it to bubble. You have several options as to the tires you choose. One possibility is to use other people's used race tires. You might be surprised at what people throw away, or are willing to sell for a very reasonable price, especially at the larger club racing events. This is yet another example of how going to races and speaking with people can benefit you. If you decide to get new tires, look for a tire that will last a long time, and don't concentrate as much on what is the fastest tire. At the time this book was written, Toyo Proxes RA-1s were excellent tires meeting these criteria. Now you need some rims. Unless you are absolutely certain that you will be using this car when you start club racing, don't purchase an expensive set of rims. Just go out and find yourself some inexpensive rims, such as steel rims, that can be found at a junkyard. This extra set can also be useful when you begin club racing. They could be used for a set of practice tires, or for your rain tires.

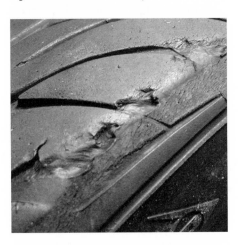

There are many things to think about before the event, and creating a pre-event checklist will help ensure you have the things you need. Below is a checklist of the typical items you should bring with you to a HPDE.

- Lots of water
- Money for event and lunch
- Club's membership card (if required)
- Helmet
- Tire pressure gauge
- Windshield cleaner
- Paper towels
- RainEx or other similar solution for the windshield
- Car shop manual
- Miscellaneous tools including: torque wrench, jack, and jack stands
- Sunglasses
- Hat

- Sunscreen
- Foldable chair
- Paper and pen
- Extra engine oil
- Brake fluid
- Spare tire (just in case!)

Because I do several events each year, I have assembled several of these items in cases ready to go. It makes things much easier, and you will be less likely to forget something.

At the High Performance Driving Event

When you get to the track, one of the first things you need to do is register and determine what run group you will be in. If registration is not open yet, use this time to get some of the other things on the list completed. One of the first things you need to do is prepare your car for the technical inspection that is required before entrants are allowed to drive on the track. The tech inspections are typically pretty basic, and if you have completed the previously-stated items before the event, you shouldn't have any problems. As a side note, when I instruct at HPDEs I also am part of the tech inspection team, so I understand what they will typically look for. Don't think tech inspectors are mean people looking to find an excuse for you not to be able to participate in the event. The tech inspectors are trying to ensure your safety.

- When you get your registration packet, a "Tech Sheet" is often included. (Sometimes this is provided when you and your car are in the tech inspection line.) Before going to the tech inspection, complete any of the items indicated in the registration packet. When in doubt, ask.
- Remove all loose items from inside the car and the trunk (such as loose CDs, a radar detector, floor mats, maps in side pockets, etc).
- When driving your car to be teched, also bring your helmet. The tech inspector will usually verify that it has a Snell or other satisfactory rating that meets the club's requirements.
- Apply the vehicle's numbers as assigned in the registration package or while at registration. Many clubs include

vinyl numbers for you to apply on your vehicle; otherwise it will be necessary to use tape or white shoe polish on the windows. Unless otherwise stated, the numbers should be put on the rear passenger side windows. If you are not sure where to place the numbers, again ask someone.

- Check the car's tire pressures. There are many factors that influence what tire pressures will be optimum for your car, such as how much the car weighs, front wheel drive versus rear wheel drive, the type of tires you are using, whether it is very hot or cold outside, and the car's suspension set-up. I would suggest that you try to locate an experienced driver at the event who has a similar car as you are driving to see what he is doing. Also, speak with your instructor and see what his thoughts are. A rough starting point for cold street tire pressures is 5 psi above the recommended stock pressures listed inside the car's door. Right after coming in from your session, check your tire pressures again. As previously stated, the most important tire pressure reading is immediately after coming in from your session. As a side note, every track that I know of has pressured air available at the track free of charge.
- Clean your front and rear windows. Having good visibility when on the track is very important.

During the course of the day, it is very important that you drink plenty of water. This holds true regardless of the weather conditions. People told me this when I first started racing, and I somewhat blew it off. Unfortunately, I learned why drinking water was so highly stressed, and I discovered that even on a cool day a person can become dehydrated quickly. Being dehydrated will lead to a decrease in concentration while out on the track and, for obvious reasons, that is not a good thing.

During the event, don't be afraid to approach instructors in between your driving sessions for some additional coaching. The instructors have years of experience that you can tap into. People often feel that they don't want to bother the instructors, but remember that the instructors are there because they enjoy sharing knowledge and seeing new drivers progress. When a student approaches me with questions, I honestly take it as a compliment. The instructors at HPDEs are not paid in the traditional sense, although they do obtain entrance to the event at no charge in exchange for instructing students. Some students think that the only reason why instructors are there is because they get free track time. That simply is not the case. When I started instructing, I realized how little the free track time factors into why people instruct at the events.

Just to reiterate, the most important objective during the event should be to avoid damage to your car while learning and having as much fun as possible. The worst thing you can do is to drive beyond your limit and risk damaging the car, or even worse, hurt yourself and/or someone else. Although some insurance companies may cover damage incurred during the school, most do not. In order to determine if your insurance carrier would cover damage, obtain your policy's list of exclusions.

Take your time building up your speeds as your comfort level increases. On average each entrant will receive a total of 1 ½ - 2 hours of track time, which is broken into three or four sessions. Initially this may not sound like a lot of time on the track, but at the end of the day you will be very tired. I still find it amazing just how tiring driving around a track is. Don't be surprised if you get home from the event and you just want to lounge around the house and go to sleep early. You surely will be drained. Euphoria may settle in the next day!

Summary of Primary Costs:
- Event Fee: The cost to participate will vary from club to club. The typical price ranges from $200 - $300. When looking at various clubs, be sure to factor in what is included in the event. Do they include classroom instruction? Will an instructor ride with you? How much track time will you receive? Do you have any work responsibilities, such as flagging, during the event?
- Helmet: You have many different options when it comes to helmets. An automotive helmet that can be used with HPDEs and club racing events can be purchased for approximately $230. If you purchase a helmet at this stage, I recommend that it be a Snell SA rated helmet so you can use it when you start to participate in club racing events. (Refer to the "How Safe is Club Racing" chapter for additional information on helmet ratings.)

- Membership in the club: Some clubs require that you become a member in order to participate in their club, while many others don't. You need to check with the club to determine if this is a requirement. Typically HPDE clubs that require you to become a member charge between $20 and $30 per year, but again this fee varies from club to club.
- Gas: Costs of gas purchased at the track versus if purchased at a gas station can be quite high. During a time when 93 octane gas could be purchased for $3.80 at a gas station, it won't be unusual to see the track charge $7.50 or more per gallon for the same grade. It may not seem like much, but it adds up quickly. The one time cost of a 5-gallon fuel jug (or maybe two jugs) is well worth the investment. The amount of gas your vehicle consumes will of course vary from car to car, but don't be surprised if the car goes through 10 or more gallons at the track. To be safe, estimate that $40 in gas will be consumed while at event. You also need to include the amount money spent on gas getting the car to the event.
- Tire pressure gauge: A good tire pressure gauge is inexpensive, and it is something that you will use often during your racing career. Make the small investment and get a good gauge instead of just buying a low quality type. (I initially bought one of those cheap convenience store gauges, and soon thereafter threw it away after being discouraged with the quality of readings it provided.) A good tire pressure gauge costs approximately $35.
- Rims: An inexpensive set of extra rims will be worth the investment. Don't be concerned with how they look or how much they weigh. Just focus on getting the cheapest rims that meet your needs. Four used steel rims can be bought for under $200 total.
- Tires: There are several factors that need to be looked at in order to determine what your tire costs will be. A general rule is that the faster you are going, the more you will spend on tires. Contributing factors are: 1) an experienced / fast driver and 2) a high horsepower car. When I first started driving HPDEs, I was not pushing my car to its limits, although I thought I was. This is also true of every other novice driver I have ever instructed. Don't get me wrong, a novice driver can

drive fast, but if you compare that with how hard they push the vehicle after more seat time, you will see a big difference. Because of this, I was not very hard on the tires initially and my tire budget was relatively small, meaning that I could use one set of tires for 10 or more HPDEs. Now that I have much more experience and push the car much harder, the same set of tires may only last 6 HPDEs. This general theory of "the faster you go, the harder you are on the tires" also applies to the other category I mentioned – high horsepower cars. A very rough estimate for novices driving an average car, using tires geared towards longevity versus using the absolutely fastest tire available, is $600 per year that includes 8 HPDEs.

- Brake pads and rotors: As a general rule for HPDEs, a set of rotors and performance brake pads should last a full season. The speeds at which you go through brake pads and rotors are also affected by many of the same principles discussed earlier with tire wear. Most cars are very easy on the rear pads and rotors, therefore shouldn't require replacement as frequently. Since the price of rotors and pads vary from one car model to another, you should go to your local auto parts store and determine these costs for your vehicle. To give you a ballpark idea, with my Prelude a pair of front rotors can be bought for under $100, and a set of very good high performance pads for $120.

- Brake fluid: It is important that you flush your brake fluid at least once a year. High performance brake fluid can be bought for $12 - $15.

Things You Do Not Need to Buy

Especially if you won't be using the vehicle for club racing, don't spend money on parts for your car other than to maintain it. You need to develop a little voice in your head that says "don't do it!", every time you consider purchasing a go-fast part. One of my friends and I will often e-mail each other our great ideas of what we are thinking about buying. All too often we both find items that are a great deal, and we wonder how we could pass up the item? The typical response we offer each other is "save your money – it is not worth it." Every time you are about to spend money on an unnecessary go-fast part for your car, consider putting this money aside for when you have a racecar. When you do get a racecar, I am sure you won't have a problem finding ways to spend your money. However, it would be a good idea to purchase some books that discuss driving techniques. Take some time and study them. There are some very good books that will prove to be more valuable and will help you reduce your lap times much more dramatically than any go-fast part. Refer to the back of this book for some suggestions.

A couple of "don't do it" items that may seem wise to purchase are lightweight wheels and cross-drilled rotors. Light weight wheels: only consider this if you are absolutely sure that this will be the same car you will be racing. And then make sure the wheels you buy are legal with the club you race with. As of 2008, SCCA's improved touring classes ITS and ITA allowed a 7″ width max.; ITB and ITC 6″ maximum width. There are also diameter restrictions as well. My suggestion is to wait until you begin preparing the car for the class and club you will be racing with. Things can and do change. For example, in 2004 my 1987 Honda prelude was classed in SCCA's ITA class that allows a 7″ wide rim. In 2005 it was reclassified to the ITB class that has a maximum width of 6″. It would be frustrating to use the car in HPDEs and spend a decent amount of money on 7″ wide rims thinking you got a great deal (even if it truly is a great deal), just to find out that you will need to purchase a different set of rims to meet the rules. Cross-drilled or slotted rotors: one of the biggest reasons you shouldn't invest in cross-drilled or slotted rotors is that they are often not legal in many clubs' classes. Instead it is necessary to use OEM rotors, so you may as well do that now.

Time Trial Events

Time trial events typically consist of two practice sessions in the morning, similar to the ones in HPDEs. Instead of having additional practice sessions in the afternoon, drivers go out on the track for timed runs. During these timed runs, only a few cars are out on the track at once (often only two or three depending upon the length of the track), and are spaced far apart from each other. Each driver races against the clock; time trials are not wheel-to-wheel racing events. Normally you will get one practice lap to warm the tires and brakes up, then two or three timed laps, and finally one cool-down lap. For the competition's purpose, only the fastest of your timed laps will count. At the end of the day, you will be able to compare your best lap time to other drivers in your vehicle's class. As with autocross and Club Racing, cars are broken into several different classes based on the vehicle's perceived performance potential.

People have different opinions regarding timed events. On one hand it introduces you to competition rules and the elements of a timed "race." When participating in HPDEs, it is strictly a learning environment and there is no formal competition. Time trials allow you to compete against fellow competitors to see who can turn the fastest lap times, without the risks of wheel-to-wheel racing. On the other hand, some people believe (including myself) that if your ultimate goal is to participate in wheel-to-wheel racing, you should focus on obtaining as much seat time as possible. Typically in HPDEs, you will receive a greater amount of seat time and more instruction than you will in a timed event for about the same price. If your goal is to race competitively wheel-to-wheel, my recommendation is to focus on events that will provide you the maximum amount of seat time and fun! If your budget allows you to do both HPDEs and timed events (if they are held on different days), then do both.

Although you are often allowed to time your laps at HPDEs, it is typically discouraged. When people time their laps they will tend to push harder than if not being timed. Many times this causes people to drive beyond their current abilities and put themselves and others in danger. Another reason why you may not want to time your laps is the tendency to become overly concerned with the times, which in turn can ruin some of the event's fun. Related to this is the fact that often timing yourself can have a limiting effect. What do I mean by this? Let's say that you hear a 1:09 lap is a blistering time. You go out and do a 1:08 – wow! Sure, that may be a good lap time, but did you do a perfect lap? Focusing on results (lap times) can easily become a limitation. Maybe if you did a perfect lap, you could have a 1:06 lap time or even better. For these reasons, I strongly recommend that you don't begin timing your laps during the first few HPDEs in which you participate. Focus on learning the proper lines, then building your speeds up gradually.

3.

How Safe is Club Racing?

It seems that one of the first questions spouses and other family members (especially mothers) ask is, "How safe is club racing?" This is a valid question, and you must be aware that there are inherent risks associated with racing. Skip Barber Racing School's book *Going Faster* contains the most meaningful statistic I was able to find on safety as it pertains to racecar driving. They quoted the research of Dr. Harlen C. Hunter and Rick Stoff, as published in *Motorsports Medicine*: "It should be safe to assume that the annual incidence of driver fatalities falls between 7 and 14. According to participation and fatality data from the National Safety Council, those rates would put driving racecars in the same hazard range as swimming, alpine ski racing and boating. Race driving would be slightly less risky than scuba diving and mountain hiking and far less dangerous than parachuting and hang-gliding."

When writing this chapter, I spoke with my wife about her viewpoint on club racing safety. Maybe I should also point out that we have a good relationship, and she does not have malicious plans for me. Her response was that after seeing what I had to do to prepare the racecar and myself prior to actually racing, she had a higher comfort level with my participation in club racing. In fact, she even went as far as stating that she is more concerned about my safety when I drive on the Mass Pike into Boston during rush hour on a business trip. When on the street, how often do you see people tailgate, cut people off, or perform other unsafe driving activities? On a racetrack you will never see someone eating, reading, talking on a cell phone, or applying makeup while driving. When I first started racing, I was approached by one of my friends who thought that it was a dangerous hobby for me to be doing. I looked at him puzzled and asked if he really thought his motorcycle riding on the street was safer than racing on a track. My point was that there are many activities people participate in; each has an associated risk which a person needs to evaluate and then make a decision if they are willing to accept the risk or not. It is important that you and the people who care about you become educated about club racing safety.

Racing sanctioning bodies recognize the importance of safety for everyone involved including drivers, crew, workers and spectators. Safety needs to be the first and foremost priority. You will find that some racing clubs have stricter safety regulations than others. When I first looked into racing, I became attracted to one racing club because of the low costs to become involved. I had some knowledge of what SCCA, NASA and other race clubs enforced for their minimum safety requirements, so I questioned what safety regulations this club had. I was very surprised with what I learned about their safety requirements, or lack there of. While to some it is great that this other club doesn't require extensive roll cages or technical inspections of the car each year, among other items, is this really a good thing?

Just as it is necessary for drivers to participate in intensive training prior to participating in racing events, many clubs such as SCCA and NASA also require that corner workers obtain training on safety standards and flagging techniques. Check with the club you are considering racing with to see how they train their drivers and flaggers. There is more to flagging than simply watching racecars go by and occasionally holding up a yellow flag. Many important messages are relayed to drivers through the use of various flags. In addition to the corner workers and safety stewards, there are also trained emergency medical technicians ready to be deployed, if need be. When trying to determine if racing with a particular club meets what you are looking for, the club's safety requirements should be high on your list of considerations.

What Types of Things are Done to Address Safety?

When I sat down and began thinking about what SCCA, NASA and other clubs do to make racing safer, I developed a much better appreciation of how conscientious most clubs are about ensuring the safety of participants on all levels. One of the first items which clubs address is the safety of the racecar itself. As discussed later in the Technical Inspections chapter, before a racecar is allowed in a racing drivers school or a race, it is necessary for the driver to have a logbook for the car certifying that it passed the thorough safety inspection. Even after this initial process is completed, most clubs require that the racecar pass annual inspections.

What are a Few of the Safety Items on a Racecar?

- Roll cage: It is necessary to meet strict specifications as to how the cage is constructed, including the minimum thickness of the tubes, mounting locations, and overall design. A roll cage is built to protect the driver from side impact and injuries in vehicle rollovers.
- Racing seat: Instead of utilizing a standard passenger car seat, the racecar must have a seat designed specifically for racing. While standard car seats are hinged to adjust seatback positioning, a racing seat uses a single-piece construction and has a fixed back. The fixed back is designed to enable the racing seat to absorb stronger forces, whereas a hinged seat may break and cause injuries to the driver. The other purpose of a racing seat is to better secure the driver, holding the person in place during an incident, and also while driving around the track, especially in the corners. The benefit of this is that the driver is able to be in better control (not sliding around the seat) and provides side support that is crucial during a side impact. Racing seats are also designed to accommodate a racing harness.
- Racing harness: These "seat belts" hold the driver in place, enabling the driver to better maintain control of the car. Unlike a standard passenger seat, a racing harness should always have a snug fit to keep the driver in place. Even the bolts used to secure the racing harness must meet a minimum quality grade.
- Window net: The window net prevents the driver's arm and hand from reaching outside of the car, which could cause serious injury especially if the car were to roll over.
- Windows are rolled down or removed to reduce glass injuries.

- Fire extinguisher: Assuming a more comprehensive fire system is not used in the racecar, a hand-held fire extinguisher must be securely mounted in the cockpit. This fire extinguisher must contain specific chemicals; not just any type of fire extinguisher will meet the required specifications.
- Kill switch: This allows a corner worker, safety worker, or driver to turn off all electrical components of the racecar. The primary purpose is to enable the engine to be shut off to prevent an engine fire.
- Removal of the steering lock: Have you ever been in a car that is turned off, and the steering wheel has become locked? Imagine if a racecar shut off while driving and this happened.

For most clubs the racing seat, racing harness, window net, and driver's suit must meet SFI specifications. Also stipulated is how often safety gear needs to be replaced. What is SFI? The SFI Foundation, Inc. is a non-profit organization established to issue and administer safety standards including standards for racing equipment. This allows people to differentiate between quality-assured products and untested products. More information about SFI can be found at www.sfifoundation.com.

Personal Safety Equipment

- Driver's suit: There are several different brands and models to choose from. When looking at driving suits, a few factors that will influence the decision as to which one best meets your needs include the SFI rating, price, overall comfort of the suit, and brand name. (The suit's SFI rating will tell you how fire retardant it is.) I recommend that you purchase a one piece suit versus a two piece suit for safety reasons. Think about wearing a one-piece suit versus a pair of pants and shirt. It is much easier for the jacket of the two piece suit to become out of place and potentially expose your body to fire. A single layer SFI-3.2A/1 rated suit: $240.
- Fire retardant underwear: Depending on the racing suit, it may or may not be necessary to also wear fire retardant underwear. Top and bottom: $90 total.

- Fire retardant socks: $15.
- Fire retardant racing gloves: As with the drivers suit, the SFI rating will tell you how fire retardant the gloves are. $40.
- Racing shoes: $75.
- Helmet: All clubs that I am aware of require that the racing helmet meet Snell's SA safety standards and have a specified certification date. What are the differences between an inexpensive and expensive helmet? The Snell Memorial Foundation states: "The Snell standards do not measure factors like comfort, ventilation, brand recognition or style, and only indirectly look at fit, weight, materials and workmanship. These are factors that frequently drive helmet cost." Anticipate spending approximately $250 for a Snell SA helmet.

The above costs represent moderately-priced personal safety equipment, equivalent to the gear I own and feel comfortable utilizing.

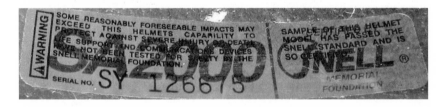

Example of an Snell SA00 Certification

Helmet Snell Ratings Explained

William Snell was an amateur automobile racer who passed away in 1956 during a racing accident. According to the Snell Memorial Foundation, his death was due to the failure of his helmet to protect him. In memory of William Snell, the Snell Memorial Foundation was formed to improve helmet design and capabilities, as well as to provide users a way to ensure helmets meet specific safety standards. Each year Snell tests and destroys thousands of helmets during the certification process. The two common Snell certifications are SA and M. The SA certification is directed toward auto racing safety concerns while the M certification is for motorcycle helmet safety. The SA certification requires flammability and roll bar impact tests, while the M certification does not. Helmets with an M certification do have a wider visual field than

SA. For helmets that have either of these Snell certifications, a label is affixed somewhere on the inside of the helmet. On some helmets, it can require that you check under the padding flaps that can easily be moved or on the chinstrap. A word of warning: Just because a helmet has a sticker on the back of the helmet with a Snell rating does not mean it is truly certified. Look for the official Snell rating sticker with the associated year's rating. When buying a new helmet, learn what is the most recent Snell certification date available. Some companies will sell a Snell-rated helmet that just became outdated by a newer certification, or is very soon to become outdated. Snell recommends that helmets be replaced every five years, and many racing sanctions adhere to this philosophy as well.

Additional information about Snell ratings and the Foundation can be found at www.smf.org.

Head and Neck Restraint Systems

As of 2008, head and neck injuries were the number one cause of racing fatalities. To help reduce head and neck injuries, several companies have developed systems that reduce the amount of load placed on the head and neck during an accident. Although most clubs don't require a head and neck system, it is something that I recommend you look into. A few manufacturers of head-and-neck systems include Isaac, Hans, and G-Force. There are several factors that determine which product best suits your needs. Factors to consider include how much it reduces head load, the product's cost, the overall comfort of the system, and the clubs you'll be racing with (check the rule book before purchasing a system). Some of these products require that the system be secured and taken off while the driver is in the vehicle, while others require being put on and taken off outside of the vehicle. Both types have advantages and disadvantages. The product that is put on and taken off outside the vehicle may make getting into and out of the car more awkward or, in a worst-case scenario, get caught on something while trying to get out of the car in an emergency situation. The unit that needs to be taken off in the vehicle requires that you consciously remove the unit before exiting the car. Any of the above-mentioned products (and others as well) would help reduce the head load in an impact, even the least expensive units. The cost for a system typically ranges between $300 and $1000.

times these less than optimum ways of performing repairs is not an option when renting.

While it can be time consuming to build and then maintain a racecar, there is also something to be said about driving a car you developed. If you're willing to put some time and "sweat equity" into the car, owning might be the ideal choice for you. And just because you won the car doesn't mean that you can't sub out some of the work and allocate your time elsewhere. If you do decide to rent a car, look at the contract closely especially the "buy out" cost that you are obligated to pay if the worst were to happen. If you do not have the financial means to cover the replacement cost, don't rent the car. Also learn how they treat repairs to any damage you do to the car, and how the fees are determined. Be sure to speak with various people and research which companies have a solid rental reputation for the type of car you're interested in renting. Not all rental companies are alike in their programs.

If you've decided to obtain your own racecar, it brings up the next decision – to buy or to build? It is much like other fundamental questions in life, such as "why are we here?" and "onion rings or French fries?" Unfortunately, these answers are not always simple. There are multiple factors that will influence your decision.

Buying a Built Racecar

If you were to ask 10 racers if it would be cheaper to buy a used racecar or build one, 9 will tell you that it is definitely cheaper to buy it and the other person is lying. This is because of an incredible phenomenon, appropriately named from the Greek term for "flushing money down the toilet": Racecarious Depreciatous. A good analogy of why it is cheaper to buy a built racecar versus building one is looking at a souped-up Honda Civic with a body kit, turbo charger, and all sorts of other goodies. The resale value of this car would be less than a stock Civic. The same basic theory applies to racecars. The typical resale value is approximately one-third to one-half of the total amount of money into the car. While this is not good for the person selling the car, it means that you can find great bargains on already built racecars. One of the best ways to find a well-built racecar is by going to the track and speaking with racers. Tell them that you are interested in starting to race, and that you are looking for a racecar. Ask if they know of anyone selling a nice one. Many of the great deals I have heard of were found by people simply talking to others, and expressing an interest in finding a well built car. In addition to talking to people, search various racing forums and internet sites (a few are listed in the appendix). When reviewing the various ads, try contacting some of the people whose ads are getting old. Maybe they have not yet sold the car and are getting anxious to sell it. When talking to the seller, ask which clubs it was raced with, when it was last raced, and if the car's logbook is up-to-date. If the car has not been raced within the past several years, you need to verify that it will still comply with the current rules. If it does not, you should determine how much work would be needed to get the racecar in compliance. Even if the seller states it is still in compliance, but simply does not have a current log book, be aware that the car will need to go through an inspection to obtain one. Ask the seller if they would be willing to accompany you at the inspection to answer any questions and ensure things go smoothly. It is not uncommon for this practice to occur.

Be wary of cars that are being sold in several pieces, such as with the motor not yet installed. Trying to put a racecar back together can be difficult, especially when you did not have the experience of taking it apart and knowing how the parts should look once together. Talk with other people about the racecar being sold to see if they know anything about it. Maybe someone will say "oh yeah, that car was fast!" Or possibly they might say "that piece of junk?" When going to look at the racecar, see if anyone familiar with racecars in the club you plan to race with lives in the general area where the car is located and might be willing to take a look at it with you. I realize that it might be tough to ask someone you don't know for help like this, but it is very likely someone would be more than willing. Where would you ask someone? There are several chat forums where you could create a post asking if an experienced racer would be willing to inspect a racecar with you. (However, if you think you may have found a good deal, you might not want to post something too specific about it in a forum or you just may end up advertising for the seller.) Remember what I said in the "A Day at the Races" chapter: Club racing is almost like a fraternity where people genuinely enjoy helping fellow racers. This next piece of advice may sound a bit obvious, but be careful that the people from whom you are obtaining information about the car are not too close to the source. If you happen to unknowingly ask one of the seller's good friends, the review of the car might not be impartial. When inspecting the racecar, it is important to verify that it will meet all safety requirements, (again, this is why it makes things easier if it has a current log book) and is legal for racing in the club and class you've chosen. Verifying that the car is legal can be difficult. It would be extremely hard to fully verify that the internal engine parts comply with the rules or not. Don't forget to bring your rulebook with you when looking at the racecar!

When buying or building a racecar, I recommend that you choose one that will meet SCCA's and/or NASA's rules, even if you don't plan to race with either of these clubs. SCCA and NASA represent a very significant amount of races that are hosted throughout the nation. Not only might you one day want to race with one or both of the clubs yourself, but if you decide to sell your racecar at some point, there will also be a much larger market for the car. As for which specific car you should choose, much of this will depend on your budget, goals, and familiarity with certain car makes. As with the other phases of racing, you need to give thought to what your goals are when buying a car.

One myth I want to dispel is that every car has the potential of being competitive, no matter what the make and/or model is, and that it comes down solely to the ability of the driver. This is not true. While clubs try to classify cars that have fairly similar performance potential together, there definitely are the cars most desirable to have, the mid-pack "tweener" cars, and the cars to avoid.

A built racecar with current logbook that is safe and legal can be found for approximately $3,000 - $4,000. A racecar in this price range will get you out on the track and you will have a great time, but don't expect that it will be a front running car as-is. You may choose to pursue a car that has the potential of being a front-runner in the future with some additional development. Or maybe you have the budget and desire to buy a car that is very well developed and already has the potential of being a front-runner. Purchasing a built vehicle with a great club racing record is one of the best options. However, be advised that just because a car has two wins to its credentials does not mean that it currently has the potential of being a front-runner. If you decide to pursue this route and are buying a car based solely upon past per-formance, make sure that it is still the same car it was when it did so well. Stories have been heard of the seller taking out some "magic" parts before turning the car over to the buyers. Even if it is in the same condition, maybe the events the car won were not typical, such as in a heavy rainstorm.

If you are working with a smaller budget, a good option would be to simply focus on obtaining a safe, legal car that is not known to be very poorly classed, but on the other end of the spectrum, will never be a front-running car as currently classified. Often times these "tweener" cars can be found for the best price and will allow you to experience all the fun of club racing (except winning).

It is better to race often in a slower, less competitive, less expensive car, than to race infrequently in a very fast, expensive front running car.

Building a Racecar

People hold mixed opinions as to whether or not building your own racecar is an intelligent decision. Financially, it is often not the smartest option, and it will definitely consume many, many hours of your time. Many people who have built their racecars say they regret it. But don't let this completely stop you! While there are downsides of building a racecar, there are many legitimate reasons why it might make sense for you. If you respond to most of the following questions with a "Heck Yeah!", maybe building a car is the right decision for you.

1. Do you like to work on cars?
2. Do you have a place to work on cars?
3. Do you already have a car that fits into a racing class?
4. Are you willing to turn that car into a dedicated racecar?
5. Do you have a "thing" for that car? (Are you an enthusiast?)
6. Do you know how to work on that car and are familiar with its idiosyncrasies (or know someone who does and would love to help you)?
7. Do you know where to get cheap parts for it?
8. Do you have a pile of spare parts for the car, or a parts car?
9. Are you a mechanic?
10. Do you have the time for it?
11. Are you nuts?

I personally was attracted to building my car for several reasons. The first was that I had an older car that would have been worth very little if I had sold it. I had gained experience driving it in high performance driving events, and I liked how it drove. The next reason was that I had convinced myself I could slowly build the car, which allowed me to gradually spend my money instead of needing to pay it all up front. Maybe I lied to myself a little with that reason, but it could be argued both ways. The best reason for my building the car was that I had very little knowledge about working on cars. Does that seem like a very odd reason? Well I did answer yes to question number 11 above. For me, building a car was a great experience. I learned more about how things in a car work than I could have ever anticipated. It was also a very gratifying (while very frustrating) experience.

If you've read this far and are still actually considering building a racecar, first you must commit to the Oath of Frugality (and actually mean it), written by a friend of mine.

Oath of Frugality
by Jake Fisher
(Read with one hand on the shifter)

"I, [your name here], solemnly swear to build my car so that it is legal in my region. I won't put any more money into my car than absolutely necessary to make it reliable and reasonably competitive.* I will strive to find parts that are used, take the time to sell off parts that I don't use, and resist the temptation to buy parts that will make the car just a tiny bit faster. I will choose tires on the basis of longevity and cost over lap time. My car doesn't have to be pretty. And most importantly, I realize that the best bang for the buck for lower lap times is seat time, and not those fancy wheels that look really, really cool."

*Reasonably competitive: A car that can compete mid-pack and does not struggle from becoming last with a decent driver.

Any money that you spend on a car, consider it money gone, and assume that the car won't be worth a dime. While this sounds like a negative, glass-half-empty viewpoint, I believe it is the best mental approach to building (or buying) a car. Unfortunately, wheel-to-wheel racing related damage can be done to a car beyond repair. And no, your insurance company won't cover damage incurred while racing, nor will other competitors reimburse you for any damage they may have accidentally caused. While building a car is stressful and very time consuming, make sure that you have fun throughout the process. If you start to get frustrated, and you will, take a break for a little while or start working on something else on the car.

In addition to developing a financial budget, you really should also develop a time budget. Like many other types of projects, it is very easy for the time line to grow two to three times the original estimate. Creating this time line is especially helpful if you have a significant other and/or children. If only I had thought about doing this! I found myself going to the garage many, many evenings right after work and busting my butt on the car. I became very focused on what needed to be completed and became too wrapped up in the car build project. The time I spent with my wife became very limited for a few months and caused a few arguments that really could have hurt our relationship. If I had been a bit smarter, and hindsight is always 20/20, I would have explained some of the various projects I had to complete during the car build process. You do not need to complete the entire project you are working on in one day; usually you can find good break points during the process. Ask how much time your family feels would be appropriate for you to spend working on the car on various days, and schedule your time accordingly. Or plan to work on a project when it won't cut into family time. Maybe your significant other could plan an evening with some of her or his friends that would allow you time to work on the car. The best solution I've found is to involve your significant other and/or children in the various projects. I have since learned this concept, and now my wife actually helps me with my repairs. How cool is that? Although she had very little car knowledge and hates having her hands dirty (disposable latex gloves are wonderful to have), she became more interested in what I was doing. I just have to make sure she feels useful – she does not like to hang out in the garage with nothing to do! Another idea may be as simple as having her or him bring something else to do out into the garage while you are working on the car.

It is now time to develop a plan of how you will approach the car build process. The primary goal at this point is to build the car to a point where it meets all safety requirements and can obtain a logbook.

Locating the Donor Car

Maybe this process is as simple as looking outside your window at the car sitting in your driveway. Or it might require that you begin shopping around. By now you may have begun to narrow down the vehicles of interest. It can be difficult, but take your time finding the donor car. Look in your local newspaper's classified ads, watch as you drive around town for cars being sold by private individuals and, of course, search the internet. Consider doing general searches of all cars under $1,000 on various automotive web sites; you might be surprised at how many options there are. When looking at the car, if there is some cosmetic body rust or the car's paint job is not the prettiest, don't worry. On the other hand, if the frame is completely rusted through or needs other significant work, it would be wise to move onto the next car. Basically, you should be looking for a car that is in good running condition and won't require immediate work done to it other than cosmetic items. If it does require repairs before it can be driven, be sure to include those figures into your budget.

Self-Inspection of the Car

Once you have your future racecar home, you should thoroughly re-inspect the car to determine what repairs may need to be done prior to preparing the car for club racing. If you are not very mechanically-inclined like me when I began, you will put the car on jack stands, take a concentrated look at it and say, "yup, looks good to me, other than some cosmetic items." While this may be an accurate assessment, you should at least begin to acquaint yourself with the car. As a minimum, put the car up on jack stands and verify that there is not a significant amount of play in the wheel bearings. To do this, attempt to move the wheel by pulling on it with one hand on top of the tire and the other on the bottom. This simple test will also tell you if there may be issues with suspension linkage. Take the repair manual(s) you purchased and start looking though them, while at the same time identifying the parts and their locations on the car itself. Typically a manual such as Haynes or Chilton will provide a checklist of items to inspect in the tune-up and routine maintenance chapter. If you identify any parts that need to be replaced, evaluate how important those repairs are. If they are non-critical parts, consider adding them to the to-do list, and take care of them later. By doing this inspection now you will have a good idea of items that need repair before they affect you in an event. You will also become more familiar with the car.

Time to Strip

Sound exciting? Well it is! In addition to the fact that stripping the car of unessential parts is a fun project, it also costs you very, very little. Before you have the roll cage installed, or take specific interior measurements, you will need to take some of the interior out. Prior to going nuts (in many ways) taking every last possible ounce out of the car, talk to others who drive the same make and model if possible and ask how difficult it is to get the car to the minimum allowed weight. While some cars are easy to get to the minimum weight. You might blow right past the minimum weight and become too light. In the case of my car, it was very easy to get to the car's minimum weight. I took out many of the basic items from the car and then had the car weighed. Much to my surprise, it was underweight. You might be wondering, "why not just add weight back in if necessary?" With my Prelude, the weight distribution is much heavier in the front of the car. Looking back now, there were some things I would have kept in the rear of the car to benefit its front-to-rear weight ratio if I had realized that the car could so easily achieve the minimum weight. Maybe it would have made sense not to have taken any of the sound deadening out of the rear of the car, or at least to have kept the rear seat in case I had decided to re-install it. Maybe I shouldn't have spent so much time taking out other fairly minor items, particularly ones located in the rear of the car. While these small items may not weigh much by themselves, they add up when looking at their total combined weight.

One mistake I made during the process was taking out the door panels very early in the build process, when I was using it for HPDEs and did not yet have a club rulebook. I later found out that it was the club's racing requirement to keep them installed unless using NASCAR style door bars, which I did not have. (A picture of a NASCAR style door bar is shown later in this chapter.) Of course, I had already thrown out the door panels. Ooops! It was then necessary for me to fabricate door panels that met the rules. I can't stress enough how important it is to know what is legal to take out, and what is not, if you value your time and money. Depending upon the club, removing some minor things such as the windshield washer fluid reservoir may be illegal.

Once you have determined approximately how much weight you want to take out of the car, it is time to get started. If you are unable to determine how difficult it is to achieve the minimum allowed weight, you can always add weight back in. My suggestion, in this case, is that you focus primarily on taking as much weight out of the front of the car as possible, as most cars tend to be front heavy. To give you plenty of room to work, take both front seats out and then begin having fun. Just out of curiosity, I put all items that I had taken out into an empty trash barrel, and at the end of the process I weighed them. I never would have guessed how much the sunroof, air conditioner compressor, and other parts weigh. Wow, it all really adds up! Oh, and be careful when taking the sunroof out if you have one. When I attempted to take it out of my car by myself, I learned how tricky it can be to take the last two bolts out while holding the sunroof up. Boink! It was a painfully interesting experience.

Before you do or buy anything, check the rulebook to ensure that it meets the club rules.

I strongly suggest that you take the major items out of the car before bringing it to the person who will be installing your roll cage. Contact the person who will be doing the work to discuss what work that you will need to complete prior to bringing the car to them. As a minimum, you need to take out the roof's insulation, sunroof (if so equipped), carpet, and rear seat. The topic of how to seal the hole that was created by removing the sunroof is discussed below. If you don't strip the car, either you will be paying the person for this work that is very simple to complete, or they will be building the cage around these items. Needless to say, if they build the cage around these items, it won't fit nearly as nicely as it would if installed when these items are removed.

When you are ready to begin taking the sound deadening out of the car, buy a basic chisel. If you are lucky and it is cold outside (the colder the better), this process will be much easier. When the sound deadening material is cold, it will break apart much easier than if it is warm. If you live down south or are doing this in the dead of summer, it will take a little bit more creativity. Many people who have done this in warm temperatures have purchased some dry ice, laid it on top of the sound deadening material for a bit, then carefully took it off the area they were going to begin working on. Be very, very careful when working with dry ice and wear thick gloves. All you need to do is bang away with the chisel and hammer.

Roll Cages

There are three basic types of cages: bolt-in cage, prefabricated weld-in cage, and custom-made cages. Although a bolt-in cage can be very tempting due to price and a basic simplicity of installation, these types of cages are not typically as safe as other cage designs. Often times these cages were designed for use with a vehicle running in a stock class where the full interior must exist, such as SCCA's Show Room Stock class. Because of this, the fit is typically not as good as other types of cages.

Another type of cage is a prefabricated weld-in cage. When speaking with companies that make this type of cage, obtain clarification as to whether the cage was designed for a car with or without the interior in it. In addition to these companies' off-the-shelf cages, many will design a cage built to your vehicle's specifications. Either way, it will still be necessary to have the cage welded in. The approximate cost for a weld-in cage that is tailored to your vehicle's specifications is $650 plus shipping. Since the parts come unassembled, shipping may not be as expensive as one might think. When speaking with the company that will be installing the cage, also talk to them about installing the window net mounting brackets. An approximate cost to have the pre-fabricated cage welded together in your car is approximately $550, which includes the welding of the window net brackets. Between the parts and labor, the total costs are around $1,200 not including the shipping of the cage materials.

The third cage option is to have a known cage fabricator or local welding shop create a custom cage for your car. When buying a custom-made cage, it is much easier to work with a shop that has experience building cages. If you do go to a shop where this will be their first cage building experience, you will need to be more thorough when describing what the club's cage regulations are, as well as any other needs you may have. Regardless of what shop you may choose to build the cage, bring the most current rulebook with you. Although the shop may have built 50 cages last year, they should review the rules to ensure nothing has changed. To find a shop that builds roll cages, search the internet, including racing chat forums, as well as the yellow pages, and certainly ask other racers who live in your general area for recommendations. When you compare the cost of a basic custom cage (without NASCAR style bars) to the other two types, it really is not a dramatic difference. Expect to pay between $1,200 and $1,700 for a custom cage including the welding of window net brackets. A SFI 27.1 rated window net and mounting hardware totals $35. When having the cage built, you may also want to consider having it built utilizing NASCAR style bars, which offer greater protection in the event of a side impact.

Roll Cage without NASCAR style bars

Roll cage with NASCAR style bars

Once the roll cage is installed, mount some high-density roll bar padding in areas your body may have contact with. When shopping for this padding, verify that it is high-density versus "standard" roll bar padding, which is not sufficient for what you need. The typical cost for a three-foot length is $15 – $20.

You should also give thought to how the racing seat will be mounted. In many instances it is possible to purchase a racing seat bracket to mount the seat to the car. Whether or not that is an option, I suggest speaking with the company that will be welding your cage for their suggestions. I had the person who built my cage also build the seat mounting bracket using the stock seat's sliding brackets.

When relying on outside vendors for your roll cage needs, begin your planning early in the building process. Also, anticipate that the time frame they provide you with will expand when it actually comes down to it. Plan your other projects so that even if their time frame doubles or triples, you won't be in a panic to complete the car build.

Suspension

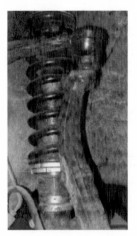

Yes, I know, I just said that the first goal is safety gear, and the suspension does not fall into this category. Yet we are discussing it before several of the other safety items. The reason for including the suspension this early in the stage is that it will take some time to research, order, and receive it. Once again, talk to other people who are racing the same car as you will be to find out which suspensions work best for your particular vehicle. These conversations will serve as a good starting point. Then you should contact a few suspension vendors. (Recommendations are listed in the appendix of this book.) Some vendors will be better than others, supplying you with a significant amount of knowledge and interviewing you as to your needs. It is important that the company knows what you will be using the suspension for. There is a big difference between a general sport suspension and a racing suspension. For a racecar, you will be looking for a suspension that utilizes a coil-over design, regardless of whether the car utilizes struts or shocks. This type of design will allow you to adjust the height of the vehicle on all four sides independently. The coil-over unit incorporates a threaded sleeve that fits over the strut and allows the perch to be adjusted either up or down.

A good company should be asking you what the car is, how much it weighs (state minimum weight plus 20 pounds), and the type of racing you will be doing (i.e., oval versus road racing). In speaking with vendors, discuss whether the strut/shock is multi-adjustable or not. Many units are adjustable so that you can modify its valving to cause it to become either "softer" or "stiffer". To get a bit more technical with this explanation, it allows adjustment of how the unit collapses (compresses) and extends out (rebounds). If it is adjustable, how many adjustment settings does it have? To very experienced people, having multiple adjustment settings are a good tool to aid them in fine-tuning the suspension. To many others, it only complicates matters. After speaking with several very experienced and reputable individuals within the suspension industry, I decided to purchase non-adjustable units. Their advice of keeping things simple and focusing on my driving, especially in the beginning of my career, really made sense. Even now that I have much more experience, I still like the fact that I don't have the option of constantly fiddling with various settings. For this reason, it is not a bad idea to purchase either non-adjustable struts/shocks or a unit that only has a few settings. The other advantage is that units that are non-adjustable, or that only have few adjustment capabilities, are typically cheaper than units with many adjustments.

When purchasing your suspension, I would recommend that you purchase the struts/shocks and springs from the same vendor if at all possible. By doing this, you will ensure that the springs you buy mate well with the struts/shocks. The price for suspension systems range greatly, and the sky is the limit. For a good quality suspension system including the struts/shocks and springs, expect to pay between $900 and $1,500. These figures don't include installation, but it is simple enough to do yourself. Often times the most difficult part of the installation is getting any rusted bolts off the stock suspension. Once you receive the suspension, resist the temptation to install it prior to completing the other safety-related projects. Installing the suspension also requires corner weighting the car, which takes time and access to scales. Maybe even more importantly, prior to corner weighting the car, it is necessary to have the other items completed that will impact the car's weight distribution. The corner weighting topic will be discussed more in a bit.

Oh, if you can't afford a decent suspension right away, don't let this be something that prevents you from building the car or racing. Sure, if you race with a stock suspension, the car won't be as fast as if it had a race suspension but at least you will be out on the track racing. I raced a little bit using my stock suspension, and I have friends who raced for a few years using their stock suspensions in non-show room stock classes.

Glass Sunroof Replacement

A standard rule in racing is to require glass sunroofs to be removed and replaced with a panel or replacement "skin". The purpose of this is to help avoid broken glass from harming the driver and safety crew, and to reduce the amount of glass that could get onto the track in an accident, especially in a roll-over. One option is to obtain a roof skin from a non-sunroof model of the car and have that installed. This is a complicated process which would take an experienced shop several hours to complete. Another option would be to bring the car to a body shop and have them attempt to weld on a piece of sheet metal, but to do this correctly is also time consuming and challenging, even for a reputable shop. One of the worst aspects of these methods is the associated cost. It could easily become a project that costs you $600 or more.

Another possible solution is to do it yourself using sheet metal. Look for a company that can supply you with a piece of sheet metal cut to the necessary dimensions for your car (slightly larger than the hole it will be covering), or just purchase a piece of sheet metal and cut the new roof skin out yourself. The sheet metal can be riveted to the car roof to cover the sunroof hole. If cutting out the cover yourself, first cut a cardboard template that is approximately 1 ½" larger on all sides than the hole which was created when the sunroof was taken out. You can purchase a piece of sheet metal from a home improvement store or online source. The approximate cost for a 40" x 23" piece of sheet metal that is .063" thick (which is typically thick enough for this purpose) is $45. If you don't already have a jig saw, it will also be necessary to purchase one that can be used to cut metal. Lay the roof template on top of the piece of sheet metal and trace the outline. Carefully cut the metal, then use a file or sanding pad to remove any sharp edges.

To find a place to purchase custom cut sheet metal, you may need to search a bit, make a few calls, and ask several places in the sheet metal business for referrals. If you are successful in finding a location, their price to supply the sheet metal and cut it to the proper size may be very close to what your cost of purchasing the sheet metal alone would be, saving you time and effort at almost no additional cost.

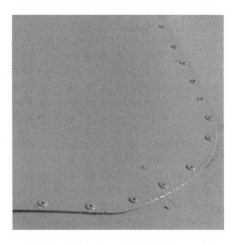

If the shop from which you purchase the sheet metal does not pre-drill the holes for you, or if you decide to make your own roof skin, drill holes approximately every inch along the outside perimeter of it. The size of each hole should be just large enough for the rivets to fit through. I suggest using 1/8" or 3/16" rivets for this job. (A box of 100 rivets can be purchased at any auto parts, home improvement, or tool store for approximately $8 and will usually state the size drill bit that should be used.) Lay the sheet that you cut on top of the roof. To help prevent the middle of the sheet from sagging and the ends from bulging, use something to prop up the middle of the sheet from inside the car such as a wooden board or camera tripod. This piece should lightly push up on the sheet to prevent the inside section from sinking in. Once you have verified that everything will fit nicely, remove the sheet and apply some clear waterproof sealer (which can be purchased for about $6) on the car roof around the edge of the opening. The purpose of this is to help prevent any water from entering the cockpit when it rains. Place the sheet metal over the covering (the edges should be covering the sealer). Now go get a helper (absolutely anyone can do this) if at all possible. Having someone to assist you with the remaining steps will make the job much easier. Starting from a hole approximately in the middle of the row closest to the rear window, drill a hole through the car roof using the sheet's pre-drilled hole. Once one hole is drilled, add a rivet. A rivet gun can be purchased for under $15. Verify that the rivet is long enough to hold the sheet in place. Before you get too far, get inside the car to verify that everything looks good (that is, that the rivet is doing its job). Now repeat the same process on the other side of the sheet (the side closest to the windshield). Work your way toward the outsides of the car, alternating sides, and making sure that the metal is as tight as possible. Take your time while completing this process. Once this is done, from inside the car apply some additional waterproof sealer between the new roof area and the existing area. It is normal for the new roof you have installed to have one or two small bulges. Remember that you are doing this yourself to save a significant amount of money.

Racing Seat and Harness

A club-approved racing seat is required for your racecar. A decent new seat that meets club requirements without necessitating a seat back brace can be bought for approximately $250, not including shipping, if purchased from a catalog or via the internet. Although some of the less expensive racing seats may not be as comfortable as more expensive ones, if you are planning to race primarily in sprint races (versus long endurance races), this difference is not very crucial. To make my seat a little bit more comfortable, I bought some basic rubber padding and inserted it into the seat below the fabric. If you look around, you might also be able to buy a nice used seat. But, please, learn from my mistakes! If you find a used seat, make sure that it meets club requirements. Yes, I am going to say it again – refer to your club's rulebook! I found a great deal on a nice used racing seat. I had the shop that fabricated my cage build seat mounts, and I installed the seat in my car. I later learned that because of the SFI certification the seat had, it also required a seat back brace. Nice. Yet another thing that I needed to have someone custom fabricate!

In addition to the racing seat, you will also need to buy a racing harness (seat belt) that meets the clubs requirements. A 6-point racing harness can be purchased for approximately $80. You will also need to purchase eyebolts and reinforcement mounting plates for the harness sub-strap(s) that cost about $4 each. For the lap belts, use the factory mounting locations and bolts for the lap belts that are very strong and already in place. It will be necessary to drill through the floor of the car to install the harness sub-strap(s). Use the reinforcement plates to ensure that the bolts don't rip through the floor, in the event of an accident.

Kill Switch (also known as an Electrical Master Switch)

Installing a kill switch is not as complicated as one may think. Avoid the temptation to over-think this process and make it harder than it really needs to be. The hardest part in completing the installation is determining how to properly wire the unit so it properly "kills" all power to the car. The before-and-after illustrations take care of this step for you.

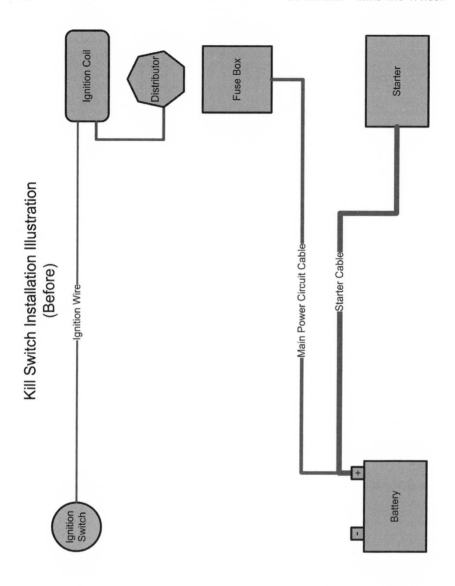

Kill Switch Installation Illustration (Before)

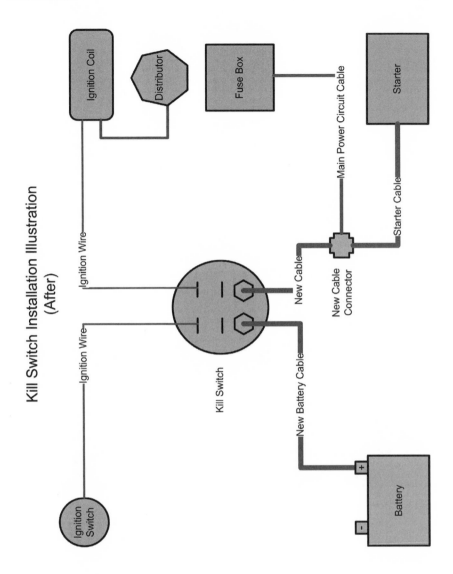

Kill switch installation illustration notes:
- For safety reasons, remove the battery connectors when completing the necessary wiring.
- When splicing the ignition wire, use 14 gauge wires.
- New cable connector – crimp ring connectors on the ends of the starter cable, main power circuit cable, and the new cable

(heavy gauge wire) that you are utilizing. Then use a bolt and washer to connect the three cables together.

When shopping for a kill switch, purchase a unit that is built to cut-off the vehicle's alternator. The reason for this is that with many cars, even though the battery may no longer be providing power, the alternator still provides enough power to keep the car running.

Once the kill switch wiring has been completed, it's time to ensure that it works properly. Start the car then turn the kill switch off. The next simple test is to turn the headlights on, then again turn the kill switch off. If wired properly, the headlights will turn off. (You may also use a voltmeter to ensure that no current is flowing to the engine.) After verifying that the kill switch operates properly, use electrical tape or shrink wrap on all exposed connections, including on the kill switch, battery, and new cable connector.

Where to mount the kill switch?

You will see people mount the kill switch in various locations. One important factor in making this decision is keeping the switch accessible for a corner worker to turn off, if need be. My recommendation is to put it inside of the cockpit. One nice thing about mounting it inside the cockpit is that if necessary, you also have easy access to the switch in an emergency situation. If you mount the kill switch inside the cockpit, again, make sure that you keep it easily accessible to someone outside of the car. While having it located near the center of the dash might be easily accessible for the driver inside the car to turn off, it makes it very difficult for someone outside to access.

Summary of Primary Costs:
• Kill switch: $35

- Heavy gauge wire. One option is to purchase an inexpensive set of jumper cables and cut the clamps off the end. $15
- 14 gauge wire: $6
- Ring terminals (6): $4
- Male and female wire connectors: $4
- Electrical tape (one roll): $2

Brake System

In racing, the car's brake system is obviously a very crucial safety item, in addition to affecting your racing performance. While stock pads may get you through high performance driving events, you need to purchase brake pads designed to withstand higher temperatures when racing competitively. When speaking with vendors, specify that you will be using the pads for wheel-to-wheel road racing, and provide them the weight of the vehicle. If your brake rotors are not in very good shape, this would be a good time to replace them as well. In addition to obtaining the appropriate brake pads, it is important that you flush your vehicle's brake fluid with racing grade fluid before driving the car on the track. The Repairs and Maintenance chapter goes into further detail about brake fluids and brake pads. The approximate cost for racing brake pads is between $135 and $150 per set; the cost for ATE brake fluid is between $10 and $15 per liter can.

Brake Ducts

Brake ducts divert air to the brake rotors which in turn cools the rotors. If the rotors overheat, the system's ability to brake will be negatively impacted. The first question to ask yourself regarding brake ducts is whether or not they are necessary. The answer depends on the car, the tracks you will be racing on, and how you drive. Let me explain a bit further.

- The car: As a general rule, the faster the car goes and more it weighs, the more the brakes tend to heat up. Again, this is just a general statement, and there are other factors that will impact this theory.
- The tracks you will be racing on: Some tracks are harder on a car's brakes than others depending on the amount of hard braking required. As an example, with my car, it is not

necessary to have brake ducts when driving Lime Rock Park (CT), Watkins Glen (NY) and Summit Point (WV). Brake ducts are necessary for driving New Hampshire International Speedway (NH). Again, this is based on my personal experiences with my car.

- How fast a driver you are: As you gain more experience, your lap times will begin to drop, and your speed will increase. As a part of this process, you will also begin braking harder, and utilizing the car's brake system more. During my first year, a driver who had a car similar to mine stated that it was necessary to use brake ducts at New Hampshire International Speedway. I responded with a puzzled, "really?" He politely pointed out that I was also going about five seconds per lap slower than him. When I started trimming my lap times, I learned firsthand what he meant.

Even if brake ducts are not necessary, they can't hurt. You don't want to find out at the end of a straightaway, while going 110 mph, that it really should have been done. Well, maybe I am exaggerating a bit here, since the brakes won't suddenly disappear on you, but they will gradually fade away.

While there are some nice prefabricated brake duct systems available for some cars, you can typically build one yourself for much less money. The first item you need to buy is the brake ducting (hose). While it may be tempting to purchase dryer ducting or other similar materials, they are not capable of withstanding the abuse it will take. If you were to choose this type of ducting, expect to be replacing it often. Instead, purchase high-temperature aircraft ducting from a racing store. This will be able to better withstand the bumps, bruises, and heat than other inferior types. The cost for a 10-foot long, 3" diameter hose is approximately $50. Yes, it is a bit expensive, but well-worth the investment. The next pieces you need are two ducts to collect the air that typically are mounted in the vehicle's front air dam. While you could purchase two racing ducts made specifically for this purpose for about $32 total, I chose a different route. Instead I bought two 3" to 4" increaser/reducers from a home improvement store for a total of $4. In many home improvement stores, this part is located in the plumbing or dryer areas.

Another piece you need are the ducts that are used to vent the air onto the rotors. You may find a race shop that sells the ones to be used with your car, but the cost will often be about $120 for the set. Once again, I used a different approach. During my next visit to the grocery store, I searched some of the aisles that have canned foods and I found some cans that were about 3″ in diameter. I then removed the ends of the cans, drilled a hole in each can, and then mounted them to the hub assembly. Although it may not look extremely pretty, it certainly does the job. This only cost me $2.50 in total, and I got a dessert out of the deal. Not bad! The last step is to complete the installation using a few bolts, hose clamps, and racers tape. I used four hose clamps ($4 total) and snugly tightened the hose to the four ducts, then applied racers tape on top of that. Using the method I used, the total cost was under $65 including the aircraft ducting.

Fire System

As a minimum, most clubs require that you have a fire extinguisher that meets certain specifications mounted inside of the car. There are also other fire systems that can be mounted inside the car to provide additional fire safety. Often times the fire extinguishers that meet the clubs' requirements can't be found by simply going into a hardware or department store. There are certain chemicals that clubs require the extinguisher to be filled with that are better suited for car fires. To find a retailer, search the internet, contact marine / boating stores, and towing supply stores. When you mount the fire extinguisher, be sure it is securely mounted in a location that you could access after taking off the racing belts if necessary. Give thought to what would happen to an unsecured fire extinguisher in an accident – it could become a projectile. The typical 2 ½ pound fire extinguisher that meets most clubs specifications can be bought for $40, plus shipping.

Transponder

Every club that I know of requires that the racecar be equipped with an AMB transponder. Prior to the use of transponders, hand-held stop-watches were used to record qualifying sessions and race results. As you might imagine, it was not an incredibly accurate system. In qualifying sessions, a ½ second can cost a driver several qualifying places. From a club's perspective, using hand-held stopwatches required several people to complete the timing and scoring process. With the advent of transponders, it became necessary to only have a few people to complete the timing and scoring process. The benefit to the driver is ensured accuracy of the lap times and race results.

This system works by using a detection loop, often embedded beneath the track surface. When a car equipped with a transponder passes over it, a signal is then sent to a computer. It provides timing information on the transponder number that corresponds to a car number in the club's database. If you are worrying about duplicate transponder numbers causing issues, fear not. The company that makes these transponders, AMB, literally has millions of transponder numbers to ensure this will never be an issue. Before you purchase an AMB transponder, I suggest that you contact the club(s) you will be racing with to verify that this is the type of transponder which they require. Every club that I know of uses AMB, but it is better to be safe than sorry.

There are two different types of transponders that you can purchase: a rechargeable transponder and a direct-powered transponder. The rechargeable transponder would typically be used for racecars that have a limited electrical system or for someone who wanted to share the unit between two cars, although I don't suggest sharing transponders. I recommend that you purchase the direct-powered transponder and wire the unit so when the car is on, the transponder is also on, and vice-versa. Using this type, once it is mounted and you have verified that it works properly, you can really forget that it is even there. It would be very aggravating to use a rechargeable unit and either forget to install it prior to the qualifying session or to have it run out of charge.

Prior to mounting the transponder, write its number down somewhere. I chose to write it on the inside of my racecar's logbook. This way it is very convenient to find if asked for the number at the track. When mounting the transponder, typically clubs require that it be located somewhere inside or near the wheel well. To mount my transponder, I drilled a few holes in the car then used sheet metal screws to secure the transponder into place and completed the necessary wiring. (The wiring process is very simple and straightforward.) After you have mounted the transponder, verify that it turns on when the vehicle's power supply is on. Then, when you get to your first racing event with your racecar (preferably at the competition licensing school), ask the timing and scoring booth if they would verify that their system receives information from your transponder when out on the track. You really don't want your first qualifying session also to be the test to determine whether it is working properly.

When it comes time to purchase the transponder, see if the club or region sells the transponder to its members. Many clubs will purchase the transponders in large quantities to provide people a discounted group price. If they don't, consider posting something on one of the racing internet forums asking where it can be bought for a good price. Maybe someone even has a used one. The full retail price of a direct-powered AMB transponder ranges from $300 - $335 depending on the retailer.

Rear View Mirror

When racing, having the ability to see where other cars are located is extremely vital from both a safety and performance viewpoint. If you look in your stock rear view mirror, the range of view is fairly limited. You really need to replace the stock rear view mirror with either a wink mirror or a convex mirror, which significantly broadens the range of view. These mirrors can often be bought at automotive parts stores for approximately $20. After purchasing the mirror, you will need to determine how to mount it. The inexpensive option I chose to install a wink mirror in my car was to purchase a few "L" shaped metal brackets, and sheet metal screws. After a bit of planning, I then gently drilled into the back of the wink mirror and into the roof of the car and securely screwed it into place. I did eventually tape the end of the mirror to the roll bar to stop it from vibrating. This mounting option was a cheaper alternative to purchasing a roll bar mount for the mirror, which costs approximately $35.

Rims

So you see some cool, extremely lightweight used rims for sale. While someday this might make sense, you need to determine if it is fits into your initial build goals. Was this something that you budgeted for? If not, stop your drooling and do what is right for your budget so you can get out on the track and race. Depending on your needs, you may not even need to replace the rims currently on the car. If you determine that you do need an extra set of rims, take your time to locate some inexpensive rims that will fit your needs. A few questions you need to answer are: what is the maximum width rim you can use, what diameter makes the most sense, and what offset or backspace will work for your requirements? Oh, what do these terms mean? Offset is the distance between the mounting surface face (the part of the wheel that contacts the car's hub when you attach the wheel) and the center of the rim. If the wheel mounting surface is further from the outside of the rim, it has positive offset. If it is directly in the middle of the rim, it has zero offset. If the wheel mounting surface is closer to the inner part or brake side of the rim, it has negative outset. Backspace is the distance from the edge of the wheel to the hub mounting surface. To measure backspace, you would lay an object that has a straight-edge across the inner (or brake side) of the rim, then measure the distance from the hub mounting surface to this straight edged object.

Prior to purchasing rims, see if it is possible to take one on trial, and return it if it does not fit properly. This would be ideal. I purchased a set of used VW rims that were very light and inexpensive, and had the rims shipped to me. When I went to verify that they fit properly, I realized that the car's wheel studs were not long enough to accommodate the rims. Doh! I then had to order longer studs, which for my car cost me approximately $100, not including labor to install them.

If you go to a salvage yard, they often have books that will tell you which models and makes have rims that will fit your car. I have also seen some similar resources posted on the Internet. And again, you can always ask other people who race the same car what they are using.

Tires

The amount of money spent on tires can add up quickly, especially if you decide to purchase the fastest tires on the market. Typically the fastest tires wear much quicker than some of the other tires available. Until you become more-experienced and decide to move on to the next step of your racing career, I strongly recommend that you choose a tire primarily based upon longevity versus how fast it is. Sure, the tire that lasts two or three times longer than the faster tire may be a second per lap slower, but how critical is that at this stage? Get out on the track and learn as much as you can. Since tire technology changes so rapidly, you should talk with other drivers to identify what brand and model race tires will provide you with the most longevity.

Another possible way to obtain tires is to visit the tire vendors at a racing event. Often times for larger clubs such as SCCA and NASA, tire vendors such as Hoosier and Goodyear will be at the track to sell and mount tires. Even if you decide not to race with either of these clubs, it just might pay to attend a race as a spectator (besides the event being fun and a learning opportunity). After the vendor takes off the used tires, most customers have the vendor dispose of the tires. To the vendor this means that they need to load the used tires onto the truck, unload the tires back at their shop, at some point bring them to a recycler and typically pay a small fee to dispose of each tire. Ask the vendor if they have any used tires you might be able to have. They will often be more than happy to give these tires free of charge. It is amazing what some people consider junk tires! Although you won't want tires that are flat-spotted, a tire that may be half of a second slower than a new tire would be great for you. Of course you also can't beat the price.

Do you need dry tires and rain tires? Ah, good question, and the answer depends on a few variables. If you are using full tread or shaved tires, these tires typically perform well in light to moderate rain. A shaved tire is just what it sounds like – a full tread tire that has the tread on it shaved down often times to 4/32". Why do people shave tires? Shaving the tire allows more of the tires' performance capabilities to be utilized earlier in its life. This process also decreases the tread block depth that ensures there is less squirm, and therefore prevents over heating of the tire. Another factor that will influence your rain tire decision is the climate you will be racing in. Do you live in Seattle, WA where it often rains 160 days each year? If so, your answer might be different than in other climates. There also are tires that are made specifically for pouring rain conditions, and due to the tire's very soft compound can't be used when the track is only damp – the track has to be very wet. When I walk around the paddock at tracks in New England, I see many people that have this type of tire. I also see that the majority of these tires have never been used and are beginning to dry rot. If you are not using a full tread or shaved tire, then buying a set of intermediate tires that could be used in various rain conditions as well as on a dry track might make sense.

Corner Weighting

Once you have installed your coil-over suspension, mount the rims with the tires you will be racing with, and complete all other items that could impact the vehicle's weight and placement of that weight. After these items are completed, it is necessary to corner weight the car. By changing the weight distribution on the car, you affect the way your car will behave when cornering. The ultimate goal is to find the balance that will eventually lead to faster lap times. When looking at corner weighting, the cross weight (diagonal weight) is the most important component. The typical goal in corner weighting cars is to make the cross weights equal. Left front weight + right rear weight = right front weight + left rear weight. Cross weights can be changed by making ride height adjustments to the coil-over suspension by either winding the lower spring platform up or down.

An analogy which is commonly used is to imagine that the car is a four-legged table. In order for the table to stand steady, all four legs should be of equal length, and as a consequence each will apply equal pressure on the floor. If one leg is longer or shorter than the others, the table will rock and thus be unstable. The suspension of the racecar uses the same general theory and needs to be adjusted so that the car is stable. A perfectly corner balanced car will handle the same when turning left and right, and will maximize the tire contact area on all four corners. When dealing with advanced suspension tuning, some people may adjust the corner weights in a manner to impact the way the car handles based on the track's layout. This approach is commonly used in oval track racing. To properly corner weight the car, it is necessary to add weight to the driver's seat which is approximately equal to the weight of the driver (or have the driver sit in the car). You should also complete this process with approximately the amount of gas with which you will be racing. A good starting point would be ¼ - ½ tank of gas. Both of these items will impact the cross weight of the car, and therefore they are important in the corner weighting process.

Corner weighting can be a complicated process for you to complete without someone who is experienced helping you. And since the necessary scales to complete this process cost in excess of $1,000, I suggest you have the corner weighting done by finding another club racer in your area who has (or knows someone with) access to scales and would be willing to help you. Or use an automotive tuning shop. Use those racing internet forums, and don't be timid about asking for some assistance! Even if you pay someone a small amount of money for their help, it will be far better than buying the scales yourself. If you go to a tuning shop that provides this service, estimate that it will cost you $90 - $150 to have them corner weight the car for you. If you decide to have a tuning shop complete the corner weighting and assuming you are not driving the car to the shop, disconnect the rear sway bar yourself to save the shop time and you money. Tell the shop you will be disconnecting the rear sway bar when obtaining the estimate.

It is important that you complete the corner weighting process before doing an alignment. Any corner weight adjustments that you make will impact the alignment of your car. If you align your car prior to doing the corner weights, it will be necessary to verify the alignment again after the corner weighting is completed.

Alignment

In the beginning, keep this process relatively simple. It is not uncommon for the proper front wheel alignment settings for one track to be different than those for another track. But, as I said, for now get the alignment setting in the general ballpark, and then worry about fine tuning the alignment when you have a bit more experience. There are three terms you need to know when discussing alignments: camber, toe and caster.

Camber is the angle of the wheel (measured in degrees) when viewed from the front of the vehicle. If the top of the wheel is leaning outward, away from the center of the car, then the camber is positive. If it is leaning inward, toward the center of the car, then the camber is negative.

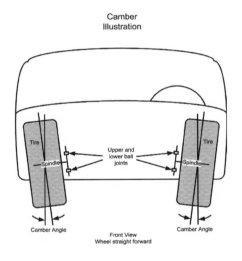

Camber
Illustration

Toe is the difference in the "across" distances between the front of the tires and the back of the tires. Toe-in means that the fronts of the tires are closer to each other than the rears of the tires. Toe-out is when the fronts are further from each other than the rears of the tires. The most important toe value is on the front wheels. Many vehicles don't allow modification to the rear wheel toe.

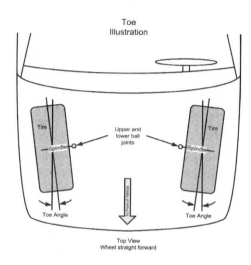

Understanding caster is not as straightforward as camber and toe. The axis that the wheel pivots on when steering is determined by the location of the upper and lower ball joints. One ball joint may be more forward than the other, resulting in the steering axis not being vertical. The caster angle is the angle the steering axis makes with the vertical. A positive angle occurs when the lower ball joint is more forward than the upper ball joint, as shown in the illustration. Conversely, a negative caster occurs when the lower ball joint is behind the upper ball joint. The second illustration shows the effect of caster on the wheel when the steering is turned. Positive caster, as illustrated, results in the wheel canting inwards at the top. This is similar to a motorcycle leaning into a turn. Note that front wheel drive cars typically don't have provisions to adjust caster.

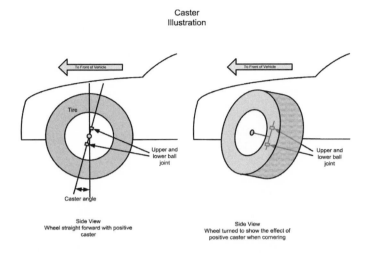

Caster
Illustration

In general, if you experience handling problems, other experienced drivers will typically be more than happy to offer some recommendations to improve the car's handling performance. There are many items that can impact handling such as spring rates, sway bar, and strut settings, etc. Do be aware that these are just their recommendations, and while one person recommends that you go out and buy a set of higher rate springs, it does not mean that is the right thing to do.

Dealing with Cosmetic Bodywork

For minor cosmetic rust or other damage, you should learn how to perform the work yourself. Even if it does not come out perfectly, well, it's a racecar. A significant benefit I obtained by having a body shop as a sponsor was having them assist me with some of the various projects on my racecar. Of course it also helped them, since I did most of the grunt work. One valuable lesson that I learned was that there is a right way to perform bodywork, and then there is the other way for a car being raced. The point is that the car won't be brought to car shows, so why spend a significant amount of time and money making the car as pretty as possible? By all means, I am not saying you shouldn't take pride in your racecar and want it to look decent. What I am getting at is that vehicle contact and off-road excursions happen in racing and the fancy paint job won't always remain perfect. Spend some time to learn how to use auto body fillers such as Bondo. If the rust is cosmetic, there are a few other little tricks you can use. For exterior rust holes where Bondo may not work well, use a piece of sheet metal and rivet it into place. When I was confronted with a few minor rust spots in the interior of my car, I used some metal tape, and then painted right over it. Again, this refers to *cosmetic* damage, not structural damage, where you need to have someone with expertise complete the repair. If you take your time doing these repairs, the result can end up looking pretty decent, and you will save a significant amount of money.

Painting the Racecar

Painting the Interior:

There are two primary methods that you can use to paint the interior of the racecar yourself. One method is to use spray paint (either using spray cans or a spray gun), and another method is to use paint out of a can applied with a brush. Each of the two methods has advantages and disadvantages.

Spray paint: You will need to worry about overspray. Everything that you don't want covered in paint must be very carefully masked. And even things that are outside of the car may get overspray on it since you will have at least one car door open when painting.

Painting out of the can: While you will save time masking the interior, it will take longer to do the actual painting.

There really is no right or wrong way to paint the interior of your racecar; you will hear different people swear by both techniques. I honestly am not sure which method I will use the next time I paint an interior of a car since both work fairly well. Regardless of which method you choose, it is important that the interior metal that you will be painting not be too cold or too hot. If you will be doing this during the winter months in a climate where it reaches cold temperatures, you will need to find a way to heat the garage up a bit either by using space heaters or simply leaving a door open to the heated house. If you are heating your garage to reach the desired temperature, allow extra time for the metal to also reach this temperature. Just because the room gets to the necessary temperature does not mean the painting surface is that temperature. If you don't have access to a garage, then it might be a good idea to wait until it gets a bit warmer outside. Read the back of the paint can to determine what temperature requirements for the painting surfaces it recommends. If you attempt to paint the car when it is too cold or hot, the paint might not adhere properly, and it may peel or bubble. I personally recommend that you wait to paint the interior of the car until after the cage is installed, although some people do prefer to paint the interior beforehand. The individual building the cage will damage the pretty paint job while installing the cage no matter how careful he is.

When you purchase the primer, paint, and cleaning solution, verify that they are all compatible. It is possible for these products to be incompatible with each other, therefore causing the paint not to adhere properly. For the driver's foot well area, some people apply a non-skid substance to the floor. I chose not to do this, and other than occasionally having to touch-up the paint in this area, I have no regrets. If you choose to do something differently with the foot well area, consider going to a boating store and see what options they recommend.

Should the roll cage be the same color as the rest of the interior? There really is no right or wrong answer. I personally chose to paint the cage a different color than the rest of the interior simply because I like the way it looks. If you choose to paint the cage a different color, in general, I found that applying paint with a brush on the cage is much easier with paint from a can. If you attempt to paint the roll bar with a spray can, expect overspray on the rest of the interior.

For the interior colors, gray is a very popular color. It does a pretty good job of hiding blemishes and dirt. Black causes the interior to become extremely hot in summer months. White is another color that many people use, but be aware it will show any spec of dirt. Depending on your perspective, this could be a good or bad thing as it will force you to clean the car often, and thus inspect it frequently. Should you use a high gloss, semi-gloss or flat finish? Again, people have different opinions, but I recommend using a semi-gloss finish.

Depending on which method you choose to paint the interior of the car and cage, the process will vary slightly, but this will give you the general idea:

- You have taken the insulation and sound deadening out, right?
- Quickly vacuum the interior.
- Using scuff pads (can be bought at auto parts stores), lightly scuff the areas you will be painting. If you choose to paint

the cage using a different method or color, you should still scuff the cage now to reduce dust inside the car after most of the interior is painted.

- Vacuum the interior again.
- Quickly wipe down the interior with a wet paper towel or cloth.
- Cover and mask the interior. If you are using the spray method, it is extremely important that you take your time with this step. You need to cover any exposed wires, as you never know when you will need to identify what their original colors were. (When covering exposed wiring, one trick is to use aluminum foil to cover it, which is quicker than taping it. I still would tape the ends of the aluminum to prevent any paint from dripping inside, just in case.) If you don't take the time to properly cover everything that you don't want paint on, in and out of the car, it will show. You will be amazed how paint particles find their way to various areas! After you have covered everything, take a break and then double check that you did not miss anything. If you have elected to paint the interior with a can and brush, this process is not as intense as spraying the interior. When taping items, use painters tape, not masking tape. If you ever need to paint over that item later, the residue which masking tape leaves could impact the adhesion of the paint.
- Vacuum the interior again.
- Carefully clean the interior, including the roll cage, using a paint preparation solvent (can be bought at automotive parts stores). Don't use brake cleaner or any other cleaner as a substitute. Once this has thoroughly dried, you are ready for the next step.
- Apply primer. Is priming the interior of the car really necessary? If you are using the spray method, you already have everything covered, and therefore it is very easy to do. Honestly, it won't cost much more money to do a light primer coat. If you will be brushing the paint on, I recommend that you at least prime the high-traffic areas such as the floors of both the driver's and passenger side. If you choose not to prime the other already-painted areas, paint a small test area to ensure that the paint will adhere properly without priming

the surface. After the paint dries, if you see cracking or bubbling in the paint, it will be necessary to prime the interior.
* Now you are ready to paint!

When priming and painting the car, start from the rear and work
your way forward. If you are spraying the interior, apply the paint in
several thin coats. If you are painting using a brush, you should at
least put a second coat on the high-traffic areas. Check the instructions
on the paint can to determine how long to wait between coats. This
sounds silly, but don't forget to paint the roof.

When priming or painting the car, at a minimum, you really should
wear a paper painter's mask and safety glasses to protect yourself from
harmful paint fumes and paint particles. Wear some old clothes and
disposable latex gloves. Not only will wearing latex gloves keep your
hands from becoming full of paint, but it will also prevent oils from
your hands getting on the metal. This oil from your hands affects how
well paint adheres to the metal. No matter how careful you are, paint
will get on you. If you are spraying the car, I advise that you to wear a
hat. I learned this the hard way and had a bit of a blue tint to my hair
afterwards. Nice! Again, take your time throughout this process – it
will probably take longer than you anticipate.

Summary of Primary Costs:
The methods you choose will impact the costs, but the following
will provide enough information to get a good idea of the related
expenses.

* Painters mask: $20 - $35 depending on the style
* Box of 50 disposable latex gloves: $4
* Two rolls of painter's tape: $14
* Can of paint thinner (cleaning hands and brushes): $6 for a
  gallon
* Scuff pads (3): $6 total
* Paint preparation solvent: $8
* Paint brushes (2): $16 total

Painting the Interior:

* Primer (4 spray cans): $16 total

- Spray paint (8 spray cans): $32 total
  Or
- Primer (1 quart can): $10
- Paint (3 quart cans): $24 total

Painting the Roll Cage:

- Primer (1 quart can): $10
- Paint (1 quart can): $8

Painting the Exterior:

If you are thinking that painting the exterior of the car will be a quick project to complete yourself, that is not the case. If you have a racecar that currently has a decent paint job, you should strongly consider keeping it as-is. Assuming that you choose to paint the exterior of the car, you have a few different options. The first one is to bring the car to a body shop to have it painted. The benefit of this option is that it involves very little work on your behalf, and you should have a nice looking paint job when it is completed. If you shop around, you may also be able to get the car painted at a low-cost automotive painting company. However, be aware that, with many of these companies, you get what you pay for. There is a reason why, when you compare their cost versus that of a reputable body shop, the price will typically be much less than what a reputable body shop will charge.

I was very fortunate to have a body shop sponsor me in my racing efforts. We had an agreement where I would do the basic prep work on the car at their shop, and they would then paint it at no charge. One day, while I was at the body shop, I spoke to the owner about these low-cost automotive painting companies. This was at a point in our relationship where he was very open with me and did not feel as though he needed to sell me on his company's work. He suggested for me to contact one of these well-known companies and ask some basic questions about the paint they use, and then compare it to what he was using on my car. Remember, the body shop that was sponsoring me didn't want to use the best and most expensive stuff on my car either. After probing an employee who worked at this low-cost painting company a bit, he surprised me by admitting that their paint quality won't match what a body shop would use. At the same time, he also pointed out the cost difference and savings his company provides their customers. Would having this low-cost paint job be better than painting the car yourself? That is something you will need to evaluate.

As previously mentioned, in the world of wheel-to-wheel racing, off-road excursions and accidents do happen. While my body shop sponsorship deal was great at first, and I learned many of the tricks of the trade, having to bring the car to them each time became very inconvenient. One of my friends painted his car using the spray paint method, and although it was not the prettiest paint job, it sure did the trick. Painting the car yourself has its advantages beyond the long-term potential cost savings. During the 2005 season, my car was a bit beaten up and needed to be repainted. The body shop that was sponsoring me was too busy at the time to paint the car, as it was right in the middle of their peak business season for the year. I evaluated the various options and decided to give painting the car myself a try. What really attracted me to this option was having much more control over the situation and not having to bring the car to a shop each time it needed to be touched up. Looking back on it, this was a great decision for me. While the car does not look as pretty as it did when the body shop painted the car, it still looks decent (especially from a few feet away). Besides, it is not a show car – it's a racecar! If you decide to attempt painting the car yourself, be aware that the process does take time, especially if you are completing the job properly. With automotive painting, the prep work is 95% of the project, and it will take several hours to complete.

If you have any body damage that could use attention, complete that work prior to any of the other painting prep work. Once that is complete, it will be necessary to prepare the existing paint surface using scuff pads. (Scuff pads can be bought at most automotive parts stores.) What you need to do with these pads is literally scuff the surface of the paint to a point when it becomes dull, thus enabling the primer to better adhere to the surface. Do this to all of the exterior areas that you will be painting. This brings up the subject of identifying which areas you will be painting. If there are areas on the car that are currently black or unpainted, such as molding or plastic mirror casings, it might be easier and/or look better if they are painted. If you have the ability to scuff the paint outdoors, that would be optimum. No matter where you choose to scuff the car, be aware that this process will create plenty of dust. Once you have completed this step, clean the car using a paint prep solvent. This, too, can be purchased at most automotive parts or paint retailer stores.

One of the difficulties in painting the car yourself is not having access to a dust-free, well-ventilated area. It seems that no matter how hard you try, something always lands on the car when the paint is wet. Move many of the larger and other important items from the garage into another location until the painting process is completed. Assuming that you will be painting the car in a garage, sweep, then vacuum the area very thoroughly. During the course of painting the car, paint dust will find its way onto just about everything that surrounds the car when being painted. An effective way to cover the walls is to purchase a roll of painters plastic at a home improvement or painting store. The painter's plastic is a roll of light plastic which can be taped or tacked onto the walls. With the use of tacks, you could also cover the ceiling, but I typically choose not to. When using this plastic, also tape the bottom to the wall or floor. This will prevent any breezes from blowing the plastic against the fresh, wet paint on the car. With the car outside of the garage, cover the floor. I suggest using a roll of paper that can also be purchased at most home improvement or paint stores. Newspaper works well, too. Cover everything! I made the mistake of not fully covering the bottom of the floor thinking that no paint would go directly under the middle of the car. Well, I was wrong. It is also important that the area be well-ventilated not only for your safety, but to prevent the "paint dust" from falling back onto the car after being sprayed. Failing to do this will negatively impact the quality of the paint job. Keep the garage door and windows open when spraying the car. I do recommend you cover the outside of the garage door as well. When painting, the garage door should be open and as I learned, overspray will get on it if not covered. Before painting the car, make sure that your other vehicles are away from the garage. You certainly don't want the paint you are spraying to land on your streetcar. To help ventilate the area further, I use a couple of fans to blow air outside. Another step that can often be overlooked is the lighting in the area where you will be working. People often believe that they have enough lighting, but once they start painting learn differently. Having ample lighting will make your painting job much easier.

When all of the above steps have been completed, move the car back into the garage and start masking and covering the areas on the car that you don't want painted. One tip the body shop showed me when taping is to quickly tape around the area, then use a razor blade to trim it to the proper size. It is also easier to tape a "perimeter" around many areas and then tape newspaper to that afterward. As noted earlier, use painter's tape, versus masking tape. To cover the wheels, a few old bed sheets or large plastic bags work nicely.

Once you are sure that everything is masked and you have double-checked the car just in case, clean it again very thoroughly with paint prep solvent. Again, as noted earlier, be sure to wear latex gloves. The primary purpose of wearing latex gloves during this step is to prevent the oils from your hands getting on the metal. After this cleaning, be careful not to touch the car with you bare hands. Next, go over the painted surface with a tack cloth to removed residual dust. This step may not be absolutely necessary, but can't hurt.

There are two primary paint application options when doing this project yourself. The first option is using an air compressor and spray gun. This method is the preferred choice if you have access to the tools, and are willing to spend the extra money, as it will produce the best results. For the spray gun, it is not necessary to purchase a very expensive gun in order to still obtain a nice paint job. I personally use a bottom feed (also known as siphon feed) style gun that can be purchased for under $60. When shopping for paint to be used with the spray gun, acrylic enamel auto paint is generally recommended over acrylic lacquer paint. (The acrylic enamel is much easier to work with.) To find the paint for this method, you need to look for automotive paint suppliers. I suggest that you mention to them that you will be painting a racecar, and ask what paint recommendations they have. You should choose a paint that is easy to work with, versus paints such as metallic and pearls, which are more challenging. The other reason to mention that you are painting a racecar is because many companies offer customers discounted body shop pricing when being used on a racecar. Maybe it is because they know the person will be there often for additional paint?

The other option is to use good ole canned spray paint. When purchasing canned spray paint, look for a brand that is made for automobile applications. When I painted my car using this method, it was necessary to make a few visits to various automotive parts stores in order to obtain the quantity of cans needed. The other option is to order the paint from one of the many on-line sources.

Regardless of which of these two methods you choose, purchase primer for the car that is compatible with the paint. Also verify that both the primer and paint are compatible with the paint prep solution you are using to clean the car. Due to time limitations I had to paint my car one year, I thought that I would skip the priming step to save some time. At first the paint went on very nicely, but as I got further into the process it started bubbling. Now that was a horrible feeling! Fortunately I was able to strategically apply decals in those locations. No, I'm not kidding. The other advantage of using a primer is that you will not need to utilize as much paint later to evenly cover the car. This is especially valuable when using an air compressor and spray gun, where the price for primer is much cheaper than the cost of automotive paint. After the primer has dried, and you have lightly sanded the car again and cleaned the surface, it is time to complete the fun process of painting the car.

Regardless of the painting method, it is extremely important that you thoroughly read the instructions on the painting products. I also recommend that you speak with the retailer you are purchasing the paint from to obtain their recommendations.

Most paints also have temperature and humidity limitations for when the product should be applied. If you have bare metal, I recommend that you use a self-etching primer on those areas before spraying the car with the primer coat. Many paint suppliers sell a self-etching primer that comes in spray cans, making this step very easy. While you could also apply a clear coat after applying the paint to make the car shine even more, remember that it's a racecar that it will get beaten up. I personally don't feel it is worth the extra money, time and effort to apply a clear coat. Especially if you are spraying the car using a spray gun and air compressor, test spray on a piece of cardboard to set the gun properly, and again each time you add new paint to the canister. When painting with a spray gun, you need to monitor the level of paint in the canister – the gun will "spit" paint as it begins to run out. One other tip is to put the car up on jack stands to allow easier access to the lower areas on the car. When using a spray gun, you may find it to be very challenging to position the gun to spray these lower sections, especially when using a bottom feed, siphon style spray gun.

Again, as with any painting you do on the car, at a minimum you should wear a paper painter's mask and safety glasses to protect yourself from harmful paint fumes and paint particles. Also wear the finest junky clothes you own, including a matching hat. Yes, you very well may have paint on you by the end of this process. As stated earlier, be sure to ventilate the area where you will be painting the car as much as possible for safety reasons, and to prevent paint particles from landing back on the freshly painted surface.

Summary of Primary Costs:
- Painters mask: $20 - $35 depending on the style
- Bondo (½ gallon can): $13
- Sand paper: $20
- Paint prep solution: $8
- Scuff pads (4): $8 total
- Tack cloths (2): $4 total
- Painter's tape (2 rolls): $14
- Painter's plastic sheeting (12' x 50'): $10
- Self etching primer (1 spray can): $12

Spray gun using an air compressor method:
- Economy bottom feed spray gun: $60
- Disposable in-line spray gun filter: $7
- Automotive primer (1 gallon): $40
- Automotive paint (2/3 gallon): $130
- Paint hardener (1 pint): $30
- Lacquer thinner (2 gallons): $16
  Or
Spray paint cans method:
- Primer (6 cans): $35 total
- Automotive spray paint (estimated 12 cans): $84

Tow Hooks

Many clubs will require that the racecar be equipped with tow hooks. The purpose of this is to make towing easier should you and the car go off the track. Many tracks have gravel traps to stop vehicles if they should go off the track. The great thing about these gravel traps are the safety and reduced damage risks they offer, as it certainly beats hitting a wall. One minor negative aspect is that the car can become a bit buried in the gravel, making it very difficult to obtain access to the factory tow hooks. In all areas, it can also make the towing process much safer, quicker and smoother. I personally recommend that you use a soft tow hook that comes in the form of a strap. All it takes is a little creativity and an inexpensive tow strap that can be bought for under $20 from a department or auto parts store. When purchasing the tow strap, you should look for one that is "flat" with sewn loops versus a rope-style with metal hooks.

Air Intake System

If you are like most racers, by this point you are just dying to buy one or two go-fast parts. If you guessed that when I mentioned this is a go-fast part that it is not necessary at this point in your racecar's development, you are correct. But if you must, go ahead and purchase an air intake system. This modification can slightly increase the car's performance (horsepower and torque). How much of a gain varies greatly depending on make and model of the air intake system. The cost for this little goodie is approximately $170 – $200.

Exhaust

For now, keep this simple and stock. If you really want it to sound "cool," put a cheap louder muffler on. One inexpensive modification that can be worthwhile is to remove the catalytic converter. This emissions device does restrict air flow and can be replaced fairly easily with a straight piece of exhaust tubing. Yes, you can do this modification yourself, purchasing all of the necessary parts at your local auto parts store. Before you modify the muffler, be aware that most tracks limit the noise decibel levels, so don't go too loud with it. If you go too loud, you may not be allowed out on the track. Louder does not mean faster.

Primary Costs:
Aftermarket muffler: $90
Straight pipe to replace catalytic converter: $7 for a 24" length
Exhaust clamps (3): $6 total
Exhaust pipe adaptors / couplers (3): $9 total

Engine

Your car's engine is another item that you should keep stock for now, even if it has a significant amount of miles on it. When I started racing my car, it had over 178,000 miles on the stock engine. Building a race engine is expensive and is not necessary at this point in your racing career. As you can see in this chapter, there are many other areas that you need to spend money on first.

Anti-sway Bar

Especially on front wheel drive cars, the tendency is for the car to under-steer (won't turn sharply enough, thus "plow"). One way of correcting this problem is by installing a heavy duty rear anti-sway bar. Anti-sway bars are simply rods of solid steel mounted to the vehicle's frame and held in place by urethane bushings. How does it work? The anti-sway bar absorbs the torsional force exerted upon the car's chassis. If you obtain a heavy duty rear anti-sway bar, it will reduce the amount of under-steer. In my personal situation, I did not drive the car with the new race suspension before changing the anti-sway bar. I simply made the assumption, based on other people's recommendations, that a large rear anti-sway bar was needed. When I drove on the track, I had a significant amount of over-steer (rear end coming loose). After further testing and having other experienced racers drive the car, I took the aftermarket anti-sway bar off and reinstalled the factory unit with urethane bushings bought from the parts store for $10. Granted, it was necessary to trim the bushings down a bit with a razor to get them to fit, but in the end it fits my needs very nicely. The aftermarket anti-sway bar continues to lie on the bottom of my basement floor. The moral of this story is, first try driving the racecar, and *then* determine what handling improvements will be most beneficial. If you do find that a larger rear anti-sway bar is needed for your car, it can normally be bought for between $150 and $200.

Other Basic Maintenance

To prepare the car for the abuse it will undergo in racing, you really should replace the basic fluids as follows:

- Engine oil
- Transmission oil (with OEM transmission oil)
- Radiator coolant: When refilling the radiator, only use a small amount of coolant and not the typical 50/50 ratio. Some clubs won't even allow racecars to have coolant in the racecars due to the slippery conditions it can create on the track. If you don't put coolant in the car, be sure to add some

if the temperatures start to approach below freezing, and add water pump lubricant to prevent damage.

Other Miscellaneous Items

During the racecar build process, there will be some other miscellaneous items that need to be completed such as removing the steering wheel lock, inactivating the air bags (if equipped), taping exposed lights on the outside of the car, inactivating ABS (if equipped), and possibly installing a fuel test port. (The purpose of a fuel test port is to allow inspectors verify that competitors are not utilizing illegal substances in the gas that provides performance advantages.) Since many of the items that you need are club and/or model specific, seek recommendations from other people who drive similar cars. Don't forget that you will need club decals, vinyl numbers, and vinyl lettering.

Note: Sample budgets are located in the appendix of this book.

5.

Technical Inspections

Most clubs have two different types of technical inspections that your racecar and safety gear need to pass. The purpose of the first inspection is to obtain a logbook for the vehicle. That logbook will belong to the vehicle for the rest of its life, even if there is a change in ownership. Then there is the annual tech inspection. In actuality, both types are similar in nature, but the inspection to obtain a logbook is more intensive and the car will be looked at in greater detail. Since both inspections review many of the same things, I recommend that you treat all inspections as if they were to obtain your logbook. This will force you to fully inspect the racecar to ensure that it at least meets the minimum safety requirements.

If you have either built or bought a racecar that does not have a logbook, it will be necessary to have the racecar inspected to obtain one. Most clubs will host technical inspections at various sites prior to the beginning of the race season. If you are thinking about bringing the car with you to the drivers' school or race to obtain a logbook, I strongly recommend that you think again. Going through the inspection to obtain a logbook is stressful enough, so why add that stress to an event? This process also takes time to complete; if you bring the car to the event, who knows if it will be completed in time for you to participate in it. If the car already has a logbook and you "only" need the annual technical inspection, I still advise that you have it completed before going to an event. If the car is being inspected to obtain a new log book, it does not also need an annual tech inspection that year. I have seen several people who thought they would zip through the line and have plenty of time before their session, only to be delayed for one reason or another. While some drivers' schools offer inspections the night before, what happens if something needs to be fixed before the inspector issues the logbook? Assuming that you are even able to get the issue resolved (and you know what is said about making assumptions), you are causing yourself unnecessary grief. Waiting until the event may cause you to miss the entire event. Have you gotten the subtle hint that I feel it is important to have this completed prior to the event?

Another possible option if you are unable to attend one of the pre-season technical inspection events is to ask if one of the inspectors living in your general area would be willing to perform the inspection at another time. Ask if they would be willing to have you bring the car to them. If you need a logbook issued, specify this up-front so that the inspector does not think that all you need is for the racecar to pass an annual technical inspection. The logbook process is more involved and requires the inspector to have a blank logbook available. Many clubs also require an inspector to have a higher level certification and training before being allowed to issue new log books compared to completing annual inspections for racecars that already have a valid logbook. It would be a nice gesture for you to bring the inspector a bottle of wine, a 12 pack of beer, or some other token of appreciation for taking the time to help you. Oh, but give the beer or other item to the inspector after the inspection; otherwise, it will appear as if you are trying to bribe them. Geez, now I must sound like one of your parents.

What is the purpose of a racecar's logbook? Safety. To obtain a logbook, the racecar must meet minimum safety requirements as outlined in the club's rulebook. In addition to the items that are reviewed for high performance events, inspectors will also usually review the following items:

- Roll cage*
- Emergency kill switch
- Racing seat
- Racing seat belts
- Window net
- Fire extinguisher
- Battery mount
- Fuel test port (if necessary)

- Stickers for the racecar (primarily the safety related stickers such as for the kill switch)
- Your full racing suit and helmet

* Every club that I am aware of requires inspection holes to be drilled in the roll cage. Instead of pre-drilling the holes and subsequently finding out they were drilled in the wrong places, bring a cordless drill with various drill bits to the inspection with you. Ask the inspectors where they would like you to drill the holes.

This list and the items you need for HPDE tech inspections cover the majority of the items that will be reviewed in a club inspection. However, it is extremely important that you thoroughly read the club's rulebook to ensure the car meets its requirements. Even if the club does not require you to bring a copy of the rulebook to the inspection, bring it with you anyway. You owe it to yourself to know the rules and where they are defined in the rulebook. Keep in mind that inspectors are responsible for reviewing many different types of racecars in multiple race categories and each one has its own nuances. An easily recognizable example is the differences between open-wheel racecars and closed-wheel racecars. Whether inspectors admit it or not, it is not possible for them to memorize all requirements specific to every type of car they may inspect. During the process remember that the inspectors are almost always volunteers who don't take pleasure in harassing you. The purpose of the inspection process is to help make you and other participants safer. In the above list, you will notice that go-fast parts are not included. Why? The answer is because these items are not safety-related, and therefore they are not relevant to this process. This is yet another reason why you first need to focus on the required safety items.

The day I had my racecar inspected to obtain its logbook was very nerve wracking. I had spent many months building the car, reading and re-reading the rulebook. I kept thinking that maybe there was something I missed. My turn for the inspection came, and overall things went very smoothly. If you take the time to prepare your car properly, there is no reason to be overly concerned with the process. Inspectors realize that you have put a significant amount of time and energy into the car. While inspectors are not "out to get" anyone, you should take as much control of the inspection as possible. What I mean is, show them your car, don't just stand around waiting for the inspector to ask you questions. Before the inspection begins, put the window net up. Bring the inspector over to that area and demonstrate how easy it is to take down. (It is not important how quickly you can put the window net up, just how quickly it will come down.) Point out to them where your emergency kill switch is located. Continue this "tour" of the car and then show them your personal safety gear including the driver's suit. What you really want to do is guide them through all of the safety items on the racecar. If the inspector questions any of these items, look at the rulebook for clarification. Don't be afraid to nicely show the inspector where the rulebook states that what you have meets the rule's criteria. There is nothing wrong with proving you've done your homework.

Clean cars and organized gear tech quickly.

What does a clean car, a nicely folded drivers suit, and well-organized gear have to do with its safety? Nothing, directly. What it does show is that you have prepared for this and take it seriously. While you don't need a fancy paint job, your car shouldn't be very dirty. Take the time to vacuum the interior, ensure that the engine bay is reasonably clean. Your personal safety gear is well-organized and folded.

How much do these technical inspections cost? The charge for inspections is usually very minimal (most often less then $40) if there is any cost at all. If you will be racing with multiple clubs, check with them to determine what the requirements are for annual technical inspections and log books. Often times smaller clubs will accept an SCCA or NASA logbook to satisfy their requirements, and thus it may not be necessary to obtain a logbook and an annual technical inspection from each club you race with.

6.

Going Back to School

Prior to you obtaining your racing license and being allowed to participate in wheel-to-wheel races, it will be necessary to participate in competition driver's schools. The purpose of these schools is to verify that you are ready for wheel-to-wheel racing from a safety aspect. You will quickly learn that there is much more to racing than simply going fast around a track.

What Needs to be Done to Prepare the Car?

One commonly asked question is, "What needs to be done to my car before it can be driven in a competition licensing school?" It is not necessary to have all of the go-fast parts such as a race engine or even a race suspension. When I took my first school, I had a stock engine, stock suspension, and old race tires. What is necessary are all of the required safety items such as a full roll cage, kill switch, drivers suit, and so on. The car also needs to have a logbook from the driving club and pass an annual tech inspection, assuming that the log book was not just issued for that racing year. If you are renting a racecar for the school, make certain it is up-to-date with the inspections and has a log book. I recommend that you review the club's schedule and identify the schools you plan to attend early in the process. You then can create your timeline accordingly.

What Needs to be Done to Prepare the Driver?

Not only does your racecar need to meet specific safety requirements, you need to as well. Be sure to thoroughly review all of the personal safety gear that you are required to have (helmet, drivers suit, etc). Most clubs also require that you obtain a thorough physical examination from your doctor. If a physical is required, I suggest that you drop off or fax a copy of the club's examination document to the doctor's office in order for them to review what will need to be done. This can be important since these exams are typically more thorough than a standard physical exam. Call and schedule an appointment very early in the process. I was shocked at how far in advance I needed to call to schedule a physical appointment with my doctor, and I have heard the same experience from others. If you have medical insurance, verify that physicals are included in your policy's coverage. Often times insurance companies only cover one physical per year, therefore you need to plan ahead. Once you have ensured that you have all of the required safety gear and made the appointment for your physical, you have some studying to do before the school.

Many clubs will actually provide you a written test. Don't worry, it is usually an open book test. Do be sure that you know the meanings of the various flags and that you are familiar with the club's overall racing rules. In general, the meaning of flags will be consistent among various racing organizations, but there may be some slight differences. Review the flags' meanings in the rulebook of the club that you plan to race with.

Basic Checklist of Items to Bring:

- Registration sheet
- A check to pay for the school (if you did not pre-pay)
- Crew
- Novice permit
- Racecar's logbook
- The club's rulebook
- Helmet
- Driver's suit
- Plenty of water to drink
- Lunch for yourself and your crew
- Sun block
- Sunglasses
- Assortment of tools
- Engine oil
- Brake fluid

- Other miscellaneous items such as paper towels and wind-shield cleaner
- Spare tire for the racecar
- Spare tire for the trailer

The Competition Licensing School

It is now two days before your first of two competition licensing schools. You have been preparing for this for quite some time now, and the day is quickly approaching. You think back to everything that you needed to accomplish before the event. Wow! There was a lot involved in getting this far, and you are well on your way to entering the world of club racing. The racecar has an up-to-date logbook, and you made sure to have its annual tech inspection completed well before the school. You hear that some people are having the car inspected at the school, but you can imagine how much extra stress that would add. If you had waited until the school to do this, who knows if you would have been able to participate or not – one minor issue causing you to fail tech and your car wouldn't be allowed on the track. All of your paperwork, a check, novice permit, logbook, and other gear are in order and ready to go. Is there anything else that you are missing? Hmm.

It is now the evening before the school. You call the two friends who are going to the school with you as your crew and confirm tomorrow's meeting time. As you try to fall asleep, your mind keeps wandering with many different thoughts. Finally! Your alarm clock goes off, and it is time to get going. The ride to the track seems like it is taking forever. As you get closer and closer, you become more anxious and a bit nervous about the day. When you arrive at the track, you and your crew members sign-in and complete the registration process. You can't help but wonder if you are ready for this. When you timed yourself doing some laps at a recent high performance driving event, your lap times were in the 1 minute, 12 second range. Then you think about what the typical qualifying times are in your class under similar weather conditions. If you posted that type of time you would have qualified in the back. You think to yourself "Wait, maybe I am not really ready for all of this? Stop it! Why am I so nervous?" You have focused on learning the proper racing line and car control before registering for this event. You also remember what you learned while reading Go Ahead - Take the Wheel, and suddenly you feel relaxed, confident, and well-prepared.

A brief warning about competition schools: The purpose of the school is not to teach drivers the proper driving line, although it is briefly discussed. The school is to ensure that, prior to competitors being allowed to participate in wheel-to-wheel racing, rookies won't be a safety hazard for themselves or fellow racers. Racing lines and basic driving techniques are best learned at high performance driving events. Some students have attended race schools without prior track experience, but it often ends up being a very, very tough day. Do yourself a big favor and learn how to drive a racetrack in a high performance driving event environment prior to attending a competition licensing school. Come to the school well-prepared – this goes for yourself and your racecar. All of this is not said to intimidate you about the licensing schools. If you feel comfortable driving on a racetrack before going to the school, then I would be extremely surprised if you did not have an absolute blast! If you are looking at your typical lap times and comparing them against qualifying times posted during a race weekend, you shouldn't be concerned if your times would put you in the back of the pack. After a few races, when you are being pushed to go faster by your competitive nature wanting to keep up with more-experienced drivers, you will gain an even better comfort level racing. You might be surprised to see how quickly your lap times drop. Take me, for example. Before attending the racing school, I compared my times to typical qualifying times. Maybe this was a mistake. It made me think that I was not ready for racing, and wondered if I would ever be. After a few races, my times dropped by a few seconds per lap and instead of running towards the back of the pack, I was running in the middle of the pack. When you go out on the track and have someone in front of you that is a bit faster, typically you will push the car a bit further, and your lap times will begin to drop. Keep in mind that the qualifying times represent the person's fastest lap of that session. It does not mean those are the lap times they are doing lap after lap. This brings up another point. Being consistent in racing is very important. Sure, that driver's fastest lap might be ½ second faster than yours, but their average lap times are ¼ second slower than yours. Guess who is going to win that race? The goal of the school for you should simply be to get through it safely, learn as much as you can, have fun, and obtain your racing license. There are no professional racecar scouts in the stands, and you receive nothing for being the fastest car on the track. In actuality, a successful race school is one where you essentially go unnoticed by the instructors. Even if you are one of the slower cars, as long as you are safe and demonstrate that you can drive the proper lines, you will be just fine.

After you unload the car, your crew completes a few minor, last-minute tasks, such as to torque the lug nuts and clean the windshield. Umm, this isn't good! For some really strange reason, the driver's side power window won't go down. Your frustration shows as you smack the window and curse. "This has never happened before!", you exclaim. One of your crew members sees you eyeing the large metal hammer and orders you to please go to the classroom session. You shake your head in frustration and walk away. When you arrive at the classroom, instructors provide you a briefing of the day and hand out some information including a schedule. When you look at the schedule, you are surprised at how full the day's agenda is – classroom session, track session, classroom session, track session, classroom session, track session, classroom session, track session. Then it hits you: There are no scheduled breaks in between the sessions. Yup, it is going to be a busy day!

The first of several classroom sessions is complete, and it's time to hit the track. While you were gone, your crew was able to get the window down without using the big hammer. During this first session you focus on your driving technique and making sure nothing stupid happens. Although one instructor who brought his racecar out on the track really tested you by getting right on your bumper, you did not get frazzled, and you made it through the session successfully. You quickly say "hi" to your crew and run off to the next class. During the class session, a few of the instructors question why certain drivers made various moves. They also said that all of the students really need to pick-up the pace. One of the instructors yells out, "Are you guys here to race? Or are you just here for a nice Sunday drive?" You think to yourself, "Don't give in. They are going to attempt to push us to make sure we don't drive over our heads and do something unsafe." In between each session, your crew knows exactly what to do with the suggestions you've given them concerning what they should be checking after each track run. The next few sessions go smoothly and you drive fast, but you don't push things too far. One driver spun off and smacked the wall, but was physically all right. After the session you see the driver load up the car on the trailer; his day is done, and he won't get signed-off for this school. Ironically, this is the driver who probably was the fastest of the group.

At the end of the day, the instructors gather and meet to determine which students should get signed off on this school. You receive your novice logbook and congratulations from some of the instructors. One of the students got signed off on both of their school requirements in this one school, but you are not at all jealous. Besides, why wouldn't you want to attend another school, even if you could have gotten signed off?

The Importance of Bringing Crew with You

When I had originally planned on going to the school, I really did not give much thought to bringing people to the event with me. Besides, what can possibly happen? I never thought twice about going to a high performance driving event by myself, so why do I suddenly need people to come with me to these schools? Fortunately, I was convinced to bring some people to the event with me. Without their help, I am not sure that I would have been able to complete the school. The window thing? That was me. I have no idea what happened that day, but all of a sudden the power window won't work. It never happened before that day, nor has it happened since. Go figure. Seriously, bring someone with you. If you think you need to find people who are certified mechanics to help you, that is simply not the case. Bring anyone who is willing to help, even if they are not mechanically-inclined. For the most part, you really just need someone there to help with some minor tasks such as refueling the car, cleaning the windshield, and adjusting air pressure in the tires.

Typical entry fee for each club's competition licensing school: $200 - $300

(Normally it requires two schools to get signed-off on your school requirements.)

7.

Race and Maintain

So, you have successfully completed a few races now, and overall things are going well, but you want to be faster. How do you accomplish this goal? It is normal to get to this point and become a bit impatient. Usually the first thing people want to look at during this stage is improving the car and making it faster. There is a common saying in racing, "First you need to fix the nut behind the wheel." It is pretty scary how quickly the costs of go-fast parts can add up, as you will learn in the Moving On chapter. It is more important to develop your driving skills first, so for now, keep racing on a budget! Too many people believe that simply throwing money into their car will automatically make them fast. Sure it will make them faster, but will it make them a better driver in the long run? If you take the time to develop these skills now, just think how fast you will be once you have a better-prepared racecar. Continue to focus on obtaining seat time and additional coaching whenever possible. If you have a choice between a go-fast part and a test day, participate in the test day. It is also important that you develop strategies on how to make the most your seat time. While seat time by itself is great, take the effort to study racing techniques, and apply them while out on the track. One can practice over and over again, but if the wrong techniques are being practiced, it won't be beneficial. Your goal now should be to develop the building blocks for greater speed in the future. Once this is completed, then you will be ready for the next step of further improving the car. To be truly successful in racing, it takes a complete package, beginning with you.

What Should You be Doing at This Stage?

When you go to races, study other drivers and what they are doing. Are they approaching the corners the same way you are? If not, what specifically are they doing differently? Be forewarned that just because someone else who is known to be a very fast driver takes a different line, it does not necessarily mean that it will also be the best line for you. The line they are taking could work better for their specific car setup, or they could just be taking an incorrect line. How do you know if what someone else is doing will help you improve your times? Ah, this is how test days should be used. Try different lines, and experiment to determine what works best. Also, don't be afraid to talk with more-experienced drivers and ask for advice. You will find that most drivers will be more than happy to talk with you. Buy racing books that focus on driver technique and the overall art of racing. A few books that were available at the time this book was written are listed in the appendix of this book. Read them! Attend high performance driving events and ask instructors to ride in your car so they can give you helpful feedback. Look for people who you recognize from the club you race with who have reputations of being good drivers, and seek their guidance. Be aware that someone who is an excellent driver, may not be an excellent coach. If you don't learn much from one driver, ask another. For some reason many intermediate or advanced drivers fail to take advantage of more-experienced drivers and miss out on the knowledge they have to share. Seeking coaching should never stop. Think about extremely successful professional drivers and how they heavily seek and rely upon coaching. Everyone can benefit from some good advice.

Instruct at High Performance Driving Events

To most people this idea may be a little intimidating, but it will prove to be a great learning experience if you choose to pursue it. Are you really ready to instruct? You have done several track events and have a good understanding of the basics, but you are far from a seasoned veteran. Take a few minutes to reflect on what it was like the first time you drove on the track. What were the primary goals at that time? Be safe, learn the basic lines, and have fun. If you are confident in your understanding of theses items, and you feel as though you can communicate this knowledge to novices, you are ready to instruct. The first time I instructed at a HPDE, I was very nervous even though I felt confident in my driving skills. The evening before the event I thought about what I should be talking to the novice driver about and made some notes. Here are a few very basic questions I ask after being introduced to novice drivers:

- Is this the first time you have been on a track? (If not, find out more information, such as how much track experience they have and at what tracks.)
- Have you modified your car? If so, how?
- What did you adjust the tire pressures to?

There are many other facets to becoming a good coach, but it is not as daunting as it may appear to be. A suggestion to increase your comfort level when you first start instructing is to find a car that is fairly similar to the one(s) you have driven on the track.

Of course, you want to know how instructing at HPDEs will benefit you. While I was a student at HPDEs, I used to think how great it would be to become an instructor, because of the free track time instructors receive. When I eventually became an instructor, I came to the surprising realization that while the free track time was nice, it was not the best part of being an instructor. It is a great feeling to help spread your passion and knowledge of racing. By instructing others, you also reinforce the importance of the basics of racing for yourself. Sometimes when people become more-experienced it is possible to lose focus on some of the little things; instructing will help you keep it all in focus.

The Benefits of In-car Video

To start with, in-car video is pretty darn cool. I found myself going to an event, and not an hour after getting home, sitting down and watching the video of what I just did. What's better than a day of racing? A day of racing, finished with watching the in-car video of that day of racing! If you think that sounds pathetic, just wait – I guarantee that you too will do it when you race with in-car video.

In addition to the racing video being fun to watch, there are several other benefits of having a decent in-car video system. Use the video you have captured as a learning tool. One of the great things about video is that it does not lie. Sometimes it can be a bit depressing when you watch the video and see the various areas that could use improvement, but these are great opportunities to shave time off your laps. Maybe you learn that you are missing some apexes by two feet, or that there were turns where more speed could have been carried through since it was not necessary to track-out to the edge. Don't be too hard on yourself about these mistakes; use your awareness of them as a tool to perform better the next time you are out on the track. While watching the video, also pay attention to what you and other drivers are doing well. Maybe you see someone make a nice pass in front of you or better yet, you make a nice pass. Now you've just witnessed practices you want to adopt into habit.

Another area where video can be very useful is if something goes wrong out on the track or if there is a dispute over a questionable move. A fact of racing is that it is possible for an accident to occur. Having the ability to review what actually happened, and provide the proof to a steward or other driver can be extremely valuable. I know first-hand how beneficial this can be. When things happen on the track, everyone witnesses the incident from a different perspective, and it is not always easy to determine which point of view is most accurate. Often times what the driver thought happened is not reality. As I said before, video does not lie.

While obtaining a video system is not free, it does not have to be extremely expensive. I do honestly believe that spending some money on a video system is worth the investment. You don't need anything overly fancy but, at the same time you don't want very poor video quality. One source for reasonably-priced, quality video equipment is ChaseCam.com (additional contact information is included in the appendix of the book).

8.

Repairs & Maintenance

In general I, like almost everyone else, really hate dealing with repairs. There is nothing like the sinking feeling after you've dropped off your car at a garage to get the service department call informing you of the repair costs. It is amazing how quickly things add up! Unfortunately, with the amount of stress racecars go through, things will inevitably wear down and break. In order to keep maintenance costs down, I strongly advise that you learn how to work on your car yourself (assuming you don't already know how to). I realize that for some people this may be an intimidating assignment – it was for me. Essentially, the extent of my repair and maintenance knowledge when I began racing included changing the vehicle's oil and brake pads. The thought of replacing an axle, or even changing the brake fluid, was beyond me. If you want (or need, as in my case) to keep your racing budget from exploding, you will be forced into learning how to do much of the repair work yourself. After successfully completing a few projects, you'll realize that accomplishing many of these repairs is not nearly as difficult as one might think. One nice thing about racecar repairs is that you usually have several days before the work needs to be completed, unlike working on a car that is relied upon for everyday transportation. That is, until the racecar decides to break at the track!

Almost all of us have experienced the joys of bringing a car to a garage. After the shop looks at the vehicle, the technician recommends the various parts to be replaced and services to be performed. Frequently these items are not necessary in order to repair the car, but are sold as items that are a part of "normal" maintenance. You also need to keep in mind that the service department representative is typically paid based on the amount of labor hours they sell. The more labor that is involved in the job, the more money the employee and garage makes. Especially in larger garages, an employee is often paid a base salary plus an additional amount on each labor hour sold. It is not uncommon for the base salary to only represent between one-third to one-half of the overall salary. Because of this, the employee is motivated to sell as much work as possible. Parts are another area where garages make money. What is the typical profit margin for parts at a repair shop? It is not uncommon for a garage to add another 40% to 50% to the price that they paid for the part. By all means, not all garages are crooks and out to stick it to you. Garages are businesses with overhead and employees to pay, and they, like all other businesses, do need to make money. Learning to do many of your own repairs will help you better afford your racing habit. Even if you don't know how to perform all of the necessary repairs yourself, next time you bring the car to a garage at least you'll sound like you know what you are talking about, and the garage will be less likely to sell you unneeded work. One good question you can ask when having work done by a repair shop is: What work needs to be done in order to resolve the problem itself – what specifically is causing the issue?

Due to the amount of fairly basic maintenance that needs to be completed regularly on a racecar, it would get very expensive quickly if you were to bring the car to the shop each time. I strongly recommend that you buy the factory shop manual for your vehicle. In addition to this manual being very detailed and specific to your car, many clubs such as SCCA require that each participant have a factory shop manual and bring it to the track. The purpose is, if there is a protest over the legality of a car after a race, the steward will be able to refer to this manual for various specifications. If you have difficulty locating a factory shop manual, speak with someone else who races the same vehicle make, or contact a dealer and ask where you can purchase one. Just to forewarn you, factory shop manuals are fairly expensive and often range between $60 and $100. In addition to the official factory shop manual, it will be helpful for you to purchase another repair manual, such as one by Chilton or Haynes. These types of manuals go into further details on how to specifically perform the various types of maintenance and repairs. (These manuals are typically available at automotive parts stores.)

So you may not exactly be a mechanic. A key thing to remember is that the big hammer you have in your tool box should only be used for special occasions! We have all faced situations when the part does not "exactly" fit, and we are tempted to "make it fit" with a little bit of help. If you reach this point, take a break from working on the car for a little while. When you run into roadblocks and are simply unable to figure out how to perform a repair (and inevitably you will), ask for advice and suggestions from other racers. The internet is a very useful tool – use it! Learn what chat forums exist for your vehicle, and become a member. If you are experiencing difficulties in completing a task, search the web site(s) to see if other people have posted information on that topic. If not, create a post asking for advice.

When taking apart more complicated parts, I find it very beneficial to take digital pictures during the process. Take a photo before you do anything to the part(s) you will be working as well as several during the process if necessary. Be sure to take the extra time to clearly label each item as you remove it. By doing this, it will be much easier when you begin reassembling the parts, and wondering "So, how does this get put back together?"

A Field Trip to the Home Improvement Store

Take a trip out to some of the home improvement and hardware stores in your area. This may sound a bit silly, but walk down the aisles and try to absorb the various items that they have. Even if while walking down the aisles you don't recognize a potential use for various items, later in the build and repair processes you may recall having seen things that might be of use. These stores can serve as a great race shop if a person uses a little creativity. One of the hard parts of this trip is to leave the store without buying some of the cool items you see. Resist the temptation unless you really need the item. It is amazing how quickly small ticket items can add up.

Brake Pads and Fluid

Due to the extreme operating temperatures of a car's brake system when being used on a race track, it is necessary to utilize brake fluid and pads that can withstand this higher level of heat. Standard replacement original equipment manufactured (OEM) brake pads and brake fluid are not usually capable of withstanding these conditions. When comparing brake fluids, the most important factor is the dry boiling point. The dry boiling point is the temperature at which a brake fluid will boil in its virgin, non-contaminated state. Brake fluid also has a wet boiling point, which represents the temperature it will boil after it has been fully saturated with moisture. Moisture will most often enter a racecar's system when the brake fluid temperature goes beyond the dry boiling point. It can also enter the system due to high humidity. For comparison purposes, many standard OEM brake fluids (DOT 3) have an approximate dry boiling point of 401 degrees Fahrenheit (F) and wet boiling point of 284 degrees F. ATE's Super Blue (DOT 4) racing fluid has a dry boiling point of 536 degrees F and a wet boiling point of 396 degrees F. There is also a DOT 5 rated brake fluid that is typically a silicone product, which can present an issue. While DOT 3 and DOT 4 brake fluids absorb moisture, DOT 5 fluid will not. Sounds like a good thing, right? The problem with DOT 5 fluid is that because the brake fluid does not absorb moisture, it results in moisture beads collecting in the brake calipers. These moisture beads can then lead to vapor lock, resulting in brake failure. Unless your car specifically calls for DOT 5 brake fluid, I recommend that you avoid it.

When flushing the brake system, it is important to completely replace the old fluid with the new fluid. Some manufactures have two different color brake fluids available, such as ATE Super Blue and amber colored TYP 200. Each car's brake system capacity will vary, but typically one liter (2 pints) will be plenty of fluid to flush the system. The price for ATE and TYP 200 brake fluid is typically $10 - $15 per liter can.

The higher operating temperatures also affect a racecar's brake pads. When the temperature exceeds the brake pads' capabilities, brake fade occurs reducing braking efficiency. Manufacturers have developed brake pads designed for racing and various operating temperatures. When evaluating which brake pad compound is right for your needs, be aware that since race brake pads are designed to withstand high temperatures, it often results in a compromise in cold temperature stopping power. (This is why it is important to warm-up the brakes during a pace lap.) I recommend that when your order brake pads, you specify to the sales representative what conditions you will be using the brake pads in, such as competitive wheel-to-wheel road racing, and the weight of the car. Whether you purchase both front and rear racing pads depends on the vehicle you drive and your preferences. In the case of my front wheel drive Honda Prelude that weighs approximately 2,500 pounds, I often use race pads in the front and OEM style brake pads in the rear. A couple of reasons for this are that the front brakes perform the majority of the braking (thus the rear brakes don't obtain as high temperatures as the front, where race pads would be needed). The brake pads you choose for the rear will also impact the brake bias of the rear brakes. Another advantage of using OEM style rear brake pads is the cost savings. Speak with other people who drive a racecar similar to yours to see what they recommend.

My preference for performance and racing brake pads is Carbotech Performance Brakes' products. Based on my experience, these pads are relatively easy on rotors, last longer than many other pads on the market, and offer great performance and feel. The company is also recognized as providing excellent customer service and the knowledge needed to match application needs. The typical cost a set for front racing brakes of Carbotech Performance Brakes' pads ranges from $130 - $150.

Routine Maintenance Timeline

The subject of how often routine maintenance needs to be performed is often debated among racers. It is a bit surprising how diverse people's timelines are to change the engine oil, brake fluid, and transmission oil is. I have heard many people state that it is necessary to change the engine oil, transmission oil and brake fluid after each race. My opinion is that doing this is really overkill and a waste of money. Think about how much it costs to change the engine oil – four or more quarts of oil in addition to a new oil filter. This adds up and creates a lot of waste. So why do people go to these extremes? The belief is that it is much cheaper to change these fluids quite often than replace damaged parts or, risk having the brakes fade during a race. I'm sorry, but there is a point when this simply becomes a waste of money and natural resources. How often do I recommend that you change the car's fluids? I change the engine oil and brake fluid after every five race events and the transmission fluid once a season. By all means this does not mean that it is not necessary to keep an alert eye on the condition of these fluids. Check your oil before each and every session you go out onto the track. The oil level should always be to the top of the full line. If the oil begins to appear dark, change it. Don't go beyond the full line because over-filling it can also damage the engine. If you feel any brake fade, bleed the brakes until you are positive that all of the air is out of the system, and make sure the brake reservoir is filled to the maximum line indicated. As precautionary measures, I do recommend that you bring extra brake fluid and the necessary tools to flush the system with you to the track in case it becomes necessary to bleed the brakes.

What are the Basic Tools that You will Need?

If you want to be able to work on your car, then you need the tools to do it. Just as a forewarning, while working on the car it is almost certain that you will come across projects that require special tools not often used and therefore not on this list. This is true especially because of the numerous different makes of vehicles. I admit it can become very frustrating having to stop in the middle of a project because you need to run out to a store to get a tool. There may also be times when you simply may not be aware that there is a tool made specifically for the task you are trying to complete. I recommend that you visit a store that sells many automotive tools to learn about the various tools available. The advantage of doing this is to be aware of what tools are available that might be of value in the future. You will find that having the right tool can make a world of difference. When you are at the track and see people working on their cars, watch to see how they are performing the repair and what tools they are using. Especially if someone is working on a car similar to yours, it would benefit you to offer assistance (for multiple reasons), even if you don't know specifically how you might be able to assist the person. Hopefully during the process you will learn something, and you will also have someone who is appreciative of your assistance. That said, the list below will provide you with the basic tools necessary for working on the racecar, and tow vehicle for that matter. With any luck you will already have some of these tools.

Basic Tool List:

- Tool box
- Metric or SAE socket and open wrench set (which depends on whether your racecar uses metric or English size bolts)
- Torque wrench (an inexpensive one works for most common applications)
- Wire stripper & crimping tool
- Spark plug gap tool

- Flashlight
- Mechanics gloves
- Jack (an inexpensive one will suffice)
- Jack stands
- Hand held jig saw to cut metal
- Tire pressure gauge
- Small mirror – No, it's not a make up mirror - it is a Racer's Mirror!
- Electric drill
- Drill bits
- Set of metal files
- Set of pliers
- Tin shears
- Screw driver set
- Set of adjustable wrenches
- Breaker bar (Two foot long "black iron pipe"). When you have a difficult bolt, use the pipe in conjunction with the breaker bar to obtain additional leverage. Be careful not to apply too much torque as it may snap to head off the bolt.

A "Breaker Bar"

- Large rubber hammer
- Metal hammer (preferably a ball end, not a claw end)
- Large metal hammer (my favorite tool!)

- Pry bar
- Ball bearing fork
- Jumper cables

It seems that, no matter how many tools a racecar driver has, we always want more toys, I mean tools. There are some tools where a higher-end version would make things easier, such as a car lift, but these are not necessary if you are working on a budget. When looking at the many tools available, give thought to whether it really is a needed tool or just something that would be nice to have. I will use the racing jack as an example. Having a racing jack would be great, but during my past five years of racing I have "lived" with a standard (and inexpensive) jack. Be aware that if you start working on more advanced projects, such as engine building, you would need to purchase better quality tools, such as a more accurate torque wrench. Not that you need any help spending even more money, but here are a few tools that can make life easier and might be worth buying someday in the future.

- Portable air tank (to be used at the track for adding air to tires)
- Tire pyrometer (probe-type, not an infrared unit)
- Cordless impact wrench
- Racing jack
- Alignment tool for checking camber
- Alignment tool for checking toe

As with all other aspects of racing, keep your eyes and ears open for any opportunities where you can save yourself some money. Take a few minutes to think about where you might be able to get your tools cheaper. I admit that for many of these basic tools, it often is much easier to go to one store and purchase the tools. If you purchase bigger ticket items, it can't hurt to look at eBay Motor's tool section, tag or estate sales, and your newspaper's classified advertisement section. For tools that you won't use often, see if it is possible to borrow them from someone you know,or a fellow racer, or rent the tools. Another option to look into is the potential of borrowing tools from a local auto parts store. Many auto parts stores have tools set aside for do-it-yourself customers to borrow. Think of it this way, if they enable you to repair the car yourself, then they also increase their parts sales. One other piece of advice I'll offer is to be creative with the tools that you have to accomplish the various maintenance / repairs. When you are at races, walk around the paddock and see what types of creative inventions and "tools" people are using. While you may not be saving what seems like a significant amount of money on each item, when the costs of all items are put together, it can provide a large cost savings.

Tool to Change Brake Fluid

One example of economizing on tools is the tool used to change the car's brake fluid. You could purchase a specialized brake bleeder tool, costing anywhere from $90 - $150. The one nice thing about some of those bleeder tools is that they allow you to change the brake fluid by yourself. Another solution is to use approximately a 12" long plastic hose, piece of wire, and an empty 12 or 16 ounce plastic bottle. At one end of the wire, bend a loop large enough to fit over the brake bleeder valve. This is done so the unit can hang from the bleeder valve by itself. On the other end of the wire, wrap it around the top of the bottle, beneath where the cap would screw on. Once the assembled unit is hanging from the bleeder valve, put the correct size wrench on the bleeder screw. The next step is to insert the plastic tube over the bleeder valve and put the other side of the tube inside the plastic bottle. Now you are ready to begin bleeding the brakes. True, if you follow my lead, you will need an assistant to pump the brakes, but the tool will cost you less than $10.

Basic Alignment Tool

Another example to economize on tools is the tool used to check the vehicle's toe alignment. You could go out and buy toe plates for approximately $55. The other option is to go to a hardware store and make your own toe alignment tool for about $15. Buy two metal bars that are at least 4" longer than the tire's diameter. (It is much easier to buy two longer pieces and cut them down to the size that meets your needs.) You will need someone else to assist you with the measuring process. Put the bar horizontally across the wheel and tire of both front wheels high enough to clear the tire bulge caused by the weight of the car. Try to get both bars at approximately equal heights. Using a measuring tape (or, if you want to be a bit more efficient, use two measuring tapes), measure the front distance between the two bars then the rear distance. When measuring these distances, make sure that both you and your helper have the bars firmly against the tire. In order to help with the measuring process, I cut two slots on each side of the bars to insert the measuring tape. You will need to pull the tape tight to avoid slack, which would throw the measurements off. If there are any items that interfere with taking the measurements beneath the car (such as brake duct hoses), you will need to modify the set-up a bit. To get toe out, the front measurements should be longer than the rear by the amount of desired toe. If it needs to be adjusted, you will need to adjust the tie rods to achieve the desired toe. To give you a ballpark figure, on many cars one complete rotation of the tie rod equals a change of approximately 1/16" toe. If the car needs more then 1/16" toe adjustment, I suggest that you try to do equal amounts on both sides of the car. Otherwise, your steering wheel may not be centered. Once you have completed the adjustment and tightened the tie rods, roll the car back and forth a few times, then re-measure the toe. While frustrating, it is pretty normal to accidentally adjust the toe the opposite way. After doing this one or twice, you will learn which way the tie rods need to be turned on your car to increase and decrease toe.

To measure camber, you will need a special tool to obtain the measurements. If you walk around the paddock at a race, ask very nicely, and possibly leave your wife and kids as collateral, you might find someone who will let you borrow their camber tool. If you decide to purchase a camber tool, anticipate paying approximately $130 for it. Of course, you could also bring the racecar to a garage for the alignment, but that would get very expensive over time (approximately $80 for each alignment).

By now you may be wondering, "What are the proper alignment settings?" There are no universal settings for all car types, tracks, and personal car driving preferences. I recommend that you speak with other experienced drivers at the tracks where you will be racing to obtain a starting point. Some of the books mentioned in the back of this book also go into detail about suspension and alignment tuning techniques.

Avoiding Expensive Repairs

Throughout the course of your racing career, things on the car will wear down and break. In most circumstances, you can get what you need by making a trip to your local parts store or salvage yard, or by scanning the internet to see what replacement parts may be available. But at some point, you may be required to make a visit to the dealership for the necessary part. It is amazing how expensive parts from a dealership cost!

During the process of inspecting my Honda Prelude, I realized that the front wheel bearing was worn down and needed to be replaced. I contacted the local parts store, but they stated that it would be necessary to obtain the parts from a dealership. I then made my way to the local Honda dealership and asked how much it would cost for a new bearing.

The employee provided me the cost of the wheel bearing – $97. He added, "Oh, you'll also need to replace both of the seals, and those are $30."

"Thirty dollars for two seals?" I replied, in shock.

"No, they are $30 each."

Ouch! For parts alone, the price was already up to $157 plus tax. Oh yeah, then there is the necessary labor to have the bearing pressed into the hub! While still in shock, I walked over to the service department to obtain the labor cost. The service technician looked up the price and told me it would be $205 plus tax, to which I naively responded, "$205 including the parts?" Nope. "Is that for both sides?" I asked, hoping he mistakenly thought I needed both wheel hubs repaired.

"No sir, that is for one side."

At that point I was speechless and very depressed about how much this would cost - $362 plus tax. "This is crazy!"

Was there another potential solution? Of course there was! I was so disappointed and frustrated about how much it was going to cost, I e-mailed one of my friends about the ordeal, at which point he simply stated "go to a junk yard and get it." I contacted a salvage yard (the politically-correct term) and asked how much it would cost for a wheel bearing. He began looking up information on the part and stated that it would be necessary for me to purchase the entire hub assembly, not just the wheel bearing. I waited in anticipation as he searched for the price…"$50 but you need to provide a cash deposit first." Wow! Fifty bucks? Nice! I dropped off the deposit and picked up the part the next day. I verified that the wheel bearing was in good shape, and that it did not have excessive play. That evening I swapped the hub assemblies, and it has been good ever since.

If you ever do find yourself in a situation when it appears that the repair will be costly, ask other racers for their advice. Maybe they will have another solution that will meet your needs.

9.

Transporting the Racecar

You have determined how you will obtain a racecar and a competition license, but now how will you get the car to the track? Yes, I know, just add one more thing to worry about. If you are very fortunate, you already have a vehicle that you can use for towing the car to the track. If you don't currently have access to a tow vehicle, then you should start giving this subject some thought. While it is technically possible to drive the car to the track, and some people do this, the better option is to tow the car to the track. If you drive the car to the track, what happens if the car breaks-down, or if it gets involved in an accident, and you can't drive the car home? How will you fit all of the necessary gear inside of the car? Again, some people do it, but it certainly is not the preferred method. When giving thought to potential tow vehicles, would you consider trading in your car and purchasing a pick-up truck, SUV, or van for daily use? Or possibly it would make sense to purchase an inexpensive used vehicle to tow with, while retaining your current daily-driven vehicle. Would renting a tow vehicle be an option? With each answer you need to weigh the pros and cons. Before making this decision, you also need to determine how much weight the vehicle needs to be capable of towing. If you choose to purchase an enclosed trailer, the vehicle choice will most likely be different than if you purchased another type of trailer. If you choose to purchase an inexpensive vehicle to use, be careful not to get something that will cause more headaches than it is worth. I obtained an old Ford Bronco that was worth no more than $600. The truck drove around without any issues until I started using it for towing. While driving to the track, it was necessary to gain a head of steam before driving up any hills, and even then it barely made it. While at the track, I often found myself worrying about the ride home instead of focusing on racing and enjoying the day. After a few races, I determined that this simply was not working, and I needed to find another way to transport my racecar to and from the track.

One option that I looked into was renting a vehicle to tow the car to the track, but most standard rental car companies such as Hertz or Enterprise don't allow customers to tow trailers. I did discover that car dealerships that offer car rental often do allow towing. Although renting a tow vehicle from a dealership was not terribly expensive, it came along with the inconvenience of having to pick it up the day before the race, then drop it off after the event. There would also be the worry if the dealership would have a vehicle capable of towing available for rental when I needed it.

Another interesting idea is to purchase a used small box truck, such as ones used by moving companies. One of my friends bought an older moving box truck for this purpose. His car is transported inside the truck, while his brother's is towed on a trailer behind it. It's very convenient. It is a pretty good idea, but there are a few concerns to be considered when purchasing a box truck. Depending on the state you live in, you may be required to have a commercial driver's license. You may also have difficulty obtaining insurance on the vehicle since the insurance company may consider it a commercial vehicle. If you are considering this option, definitely contact your insurance agent to determine what your state's related motor vehicle laws are prior to purchasing a box truck. The other concern is how the racecar is loaded into the truck. Each time I watch my friend either put the car into the truck, or take it out, it becomes a bit nerve-racking even for me as an onlooker. Think about the height difference between a car coming off a trailer, versus what it would be like using a box truck.

After considering all possible options, my wife and I decided to sell one of our daily-driven cars and purchase a Toyota Tundra pick-up truck. This decision was extremely difficult for, me since we were selling the car I had wanted for many years, my "baby." Yes, it was the Mitsubishi 3000GT that I mentioned in the Getting Your Feet Wet chapter. Looking back on the decision now, it really made sense based on my racing goals. Having a reliable tow vehicle made racing more enjoyable and took away much of my previous stress.

If you decide not to turn your daily-driven car into a tow vehicle, you can find an inexpensive tow vehicle that will still be fairly reliable.

Do be careful not to purchase a tow vehicle that will require constant repairs. Take your time and look around for something that suits your current and future needs. For example, you may want to purchase a vehicle that is capable of towing a "full" trailer, even if you only intend to utilize a tow dolly for now. You may consider purchasing a utility van – they can make excellent tow vehicles, and used ones can be bought relatively inexpensively. When I did some quick searches for vans, SUVs, and pick-up trucks, I was positively surprised at what could be found for under $2,500.

Once you obtain a tow vehicle, it will be necessary to install a receiver hitch, if it does not already have one on it. When purchasing a receiver hitch, it is very important to choose the correct class receiver (amount of weight it can support) based on your towing needs. The gross towing weight and tongue weight will determine the hitch needed. The gross towing weight is the weight of the trailer fully loaded and ready for towing. The tongue weight is the downward push exerted on the hitch ball by the trailer coupler. When looking at the gross towing weight and tongue weight, take into consideration all of the tools, race tires and other items that may be loaded on the trailer. For safety reasons, don't exceed the rating of any component in your towing system (tow vehicle, receiver hitch, ball mount, and ball). A typical custom-fit receiver hitch costs $120 - $150. Since receiver hitches are made to fit specific vehicles, the installation process is often much easier than one might think. However, it still might be a good idea to contact a trailer dealer or moving company (such as U-Haul) to see how much they would charge for a receiver hitch and installation. In addition to the hitch, you will also need a trailer ball which mounts on the receiver hitch. Be sure of the ball size the trailer requires, as one size won't be compatible with all trailers. A trailer ball can be bought for approximately $12. Depending on the trailer you choose, it may also be necessary to convert the plug from 4 pins to 7 pins. Don't cut the 4 pin connector off, as it is nice to have just in case you ever tow something else. Think more toys! A pin adaptor typically costs less than $20.

Trailer Options

You now need to determine the type of trailer that is right for you. There are a several different types of trailers to choose from that come in many different shapes and sizes. Later in this chapter is a list that includes approximate weights for several common types of trailers when completely empty and "stock" (before items such as tire racks are added). If you plan to add additional accessories such as a tire rack or storage compartment, you also need to consider the overall size of the trailer to accommodate these items as well as added weight. Trailer weight and pricing will vary among manufacturers and retailers, but at least the information below will provide you an idea of the relative costs.

Tow Dolly

Although most racers do not use tow dollies (though I have been using one for several years now), there are some advantages to it. Possibly the best things about a tow dolly are the price, size, and weight. Because they are so light, they can easily be moved around by hand, unlike a full-sized trailer. The weight of a dolly also increases the potential tow vehicle choices available to utilize, since some may not be capable of towing heavier trailers. Another benefit is that a tow dolly requires little maintenance, primarily because it typically does not have brakes. Depending on your state's motor vehicle laws, you may not be required to register the tow dolly, thus saving you money each year, as compared to a trailer.

What are some of the disadvantages? Most people using tow dollies have front wheel drive cars, although I have seen many rear wheel drive cars on tow dollies. In order to utilize a tow dolly with a rear wheel drive car, it will be necessary to back the car onto the trailer and strap the steering wheel so it does not move. I personally don't believe it is a very safe practice. What happens if the strap comes loose? It is not a pleasant thought.

If a tow dolly is used, some states require that the vehicle being towed be registered and assigned license plates. If the racecar must be registered, then you should determine if it is also necessary for the racecar to pass emissions testing. Another disadvantage of using a tow dolly is transporting the racecar home if it becomes damaged at the track in a way that impacts its ability to have two wheels on the road. One other minor item is that, when a car is loaded onto a tow dolly, it is not possible to back-up more than a few feet. The reason for this is that the dolly's platform (where the car wheels sit) pivots to enable the trailer to be capable of turning. Also, if you choose to utilize a tow dolly, it will be necessary to have two rims with street tires mounted on them for use when transporting the racecar, so that you won't wear down your race tires. A tow dolly:

- Weighs approximately 500 pounds.
- Costs approximately $1,100 new

Open and Enclosed Trailers

There are several types of open and enclosed trailers that share benefits and disadvantages as compared to a tow dolly. One especially nice feature of open and enclosed trailers is that the racecar is off the road and resting on the trailer during transit. If damage occurs to the racecar, the chances of being able to get the racecar home are much greater compared to when using a tow dolly.

An open trailer with runways is typically less expensive and weighs less than its counterparts. But depending on what other uses you may have for a trailer, a full-deck or enclosed trailer can prove to be useful in other ways at home. Yeah, of course you need a full-deck trailer for your home landscaping needs. At least that's one excuse I've tried using before. It is also possible to add accessories, (such as a tire rack and storage box), to open trailers, which can be very useful.

Enclosed trailers can be outfitted with many, many different accessories that are securely locked inside the trailer. For many people it becomes a rolling garage and/or motel room. Remember that all of the goodies being transported in the trailer add up in weight. Enclosed trailers are tougher to tow because of the heavier weight, more obstructed view, and overall size. Keep in mind when looking at the enclosed trailer's weight, that this represents the empty weight. If you have an enclosed trailer, you will end up storing many items in the trailer that will add to the total weight of the trailer. The listing below represents approximate weights and pricing for new trailers. Please be aware that pricing for trailers can vary considerably among trailer dealers.

Open trailer made of steel with runways

- A 21' trailer weighs approximately 1,750 pounds
- Costs approximately $2,000 new

Open trailer made of aluminum with runways
- A 21' trailer weighs approximately 1,100
- Costs approximately $4,800

Open trailer made of steel with a full-deck

- A 21' trailer weighs approximately 2,250 pounds
- Costs approximately $2,500 new

Open trailer made of wood with a full-deck
- A 21' trailer weighs approximately 1,850 pounds
- Costs approximately $2,900 new

Open trailer made of aluminum with a full-deck
- A 21' trailer weighs approximately 1,500 pounds
- Costs approximately $5,200 new

Enclosed trailer

- A 22' trailer weighs approximately 3,400 pounds
- Costs approximately $6,800 new

Note: The above-stated lengths represent the total length of the trailer, including the tongue.

If you choose to purchase an open trailer, you will also need to determine which type of brakes it will be equipped with. There are two different types of trailer brake systems – surge brakes and electric brakes. Surge brakes are a totally trailer self-contained braking system on the trailer that requires no electrical, hydraulic or other components connected to the tow vehicle for operation of the trailer brakes. Instead, the inertial differential pressure that is developed between the tow vehicle and trailer during braking activates the brakes. This creates a mechanical pressure that causes the trailer brakes to be applied in proportion to the amount of braking being applied by the tow vehicle. One unintended consequence is that if you back the trailer up a hill, the surge brakes will usually activate, making the process a bit harder.

Electric brakes utilize a system that is tied into the tow vehicle's brake system through an actuator. An actuator sends the braking information that the tow vehicle is undergoing to the trailer brakes. One nice feature of using electric brakes with an actuator is that you can adjust the amount of braking the trailer does when the trailer brakes are activated. If the trailer begins to "wag" (move from side to side), the brake actuator can be manually applied to straighten things out. The other major benefit of electric brakes is that there is no delay in braking response, unlike surge brakes. As you may have gathered from what was said above, to use electric brakes it is necessary that the tow vehicle have an actuator installed in it. Most actuators are about the size of a radar detector and can be mounted in a way that allows it to be removed from the vehicle when not being used. For many vehicles, it is possible to purchase an adaptor that helps make the actuator installation much easier. Essentially, to install an actuator if an adaptor is not available, you must tie into the tow vehicle's brake light wire and a power source. The typical price that auto part stores sell universal actuators for is between $50 and $100. The price for an adaptor unit (if one is made for your vehicle) varies, but is usually less than $30.

Regardless of which brake system you utilize, for safety reasons I strongly suggest that you buy a trailer with a four-wheel brake system. If you are thinking of purchasing a trailer that utilizes a two-wheel brake system, verify with the state you are registering it with to see if it will even meet the state's regulations. The one exception to this is with a tow dolly. Because a tow dolly is extremely light, it is not necessary to have trailer brakes.

If the trailer you purchase utilizes brakes, it will be another item that you will need to inspect regularly and maintain.

Where to Find Used Trailers

Used trailers typically don't depreciate very quickly, but purchasing one can still provide a cost savings. A used tow dolly typically can be bought for about $500. A nice, used open deck steel trailer can be found for about $1,200. Used enclosed trailers have a large range in pricing, but a used 22' trailer can be found for approximately $4,500. The key is to take your time finding a trailer in nice condition at a reasonable price. If you decide to purchase a used trailer, make sure that the brakes and all electrical components are in good working order. If the trailer tires need to be replaced soon, factor that into the pricing. There are many places where good used trailers are advertised. Look at local newspapers, eBay, various internet racing forums, and RV dealerships. Also, ask fellow racers if they know of any good deals.

When pricing new and used trailers, consider what other items are being included and what items will be necessary for you to purchase.

- A spare wheel and tire for the trailer is an absolute must! $55
- D-ring tie down brackets (to secure your racecar to the trailer). Four D-rings total $40
- Tie down straps. Four total $60 - $80
- A tire rack. Consider having someone fabricate one for you.
- Trailer coupler lock (so no one can steal your nice trailer). $30
- Also, don't forget about your state's registration, taxes, and insurance costs if applicable.

10.

Moving On

The eternal question in club racing: What does it take to become a front-runner? People try to pinpoint the few qualities that it takes to run up front, but it really consists of a total package. Yup, you guessed it – you are the package's core. Throughout this book, I continuously stress how important it is to develop and refine your driving skills. There are multiple reasons for this philosophy. The first reason is because improving your racing skills does not have to be extremely expensive. The other reason is that once you have the necessary skills, you will find obtaining the car that enables you to reach this next level to be the easy part. By all means, when I say "the easy part," it is not to say that coming up with the funding is simple. What it means is that people can't buy their way into becoming a great driver; this takes more work than simply buying the right racecar.

Take some time and revisit your racing goals to determine if you are willing to put in the time, effort, and money to become a front-runner. While everyone wants to win races, there is absolutely nothing wrong with not being a front-runner. I look back at some of my previous races and just how much fun I had running mid-pack. I developed a pretty intense (yet fun) rivalry with a friend I met through racing. It was not uncommon for us to qualify within 0.05 of a second of each other and be less than three cars apart during the entire race. Jake Fisher, the other driver, often joked that he thought I would rather finish in 18th place and beat him than finish second and lose only to him. All right, so he might have been correct. I have also been fortunate enough to experience what it is like to be a front-runner. Am I necessarily having more fun? Honestly, I am not sure. My first race win was awesome! It is something that I will always remember and cherish. I remember finishing the race and thinking to myself "Did I really win this?" While driving up to the worker who carried out the checkered flag for the victory lap, I couldn't help but think "How embarrassing will this be if I actually came in second place?" Of course I knew that I had won, but it just didn't seem like reality. At the same time, racing has become much, much more expensive for me. Just ask my wife!

Before you can become a front-runner in a competitive class, you will need to ensure that both you and the car are ready for the challenge. Of course, I will start with what needs to be done to you, the driver, before talking about what needs to be done to the car. I hear many people consistently make excuses why they can't win despite the fact that they have a well-developed car with the potential to run up-front. I will say that it certainly is much easier to blame the car than yourself. The reason they are not winning is often because they have not spent the necessary time and effort on developing themselves yet. Do you remember those books I previously recommended on driving techniques? Read them, then re-read them. Once you have done that, read them one more time. You may be surprised with what you pick up from the books as your perspective changes after gaining more experience. Depending on which books you bought, it may be worthwhile to see what other racing techniques and racecar tuning books are available. In addition to referring to the appendix of this book, talk with other drivers to see what other new books have been published recently that they recommend.

Do you have the heart, will, and determination to win?

The Mental Aspects of Racing

Mentally, you need to get yourself ready to win. Close your eyes, relax, and take a few deep breaths. Picture yourself at the end of the race crossing the finish line. No really – put the book down for a moment and try it.

What place did you finish in? You need to be able to visualize yourself crossing the finish line and winning. If you don't believe you have the possibility of winning races, you most likely won't win. Taking it a bit further, if you see yourself as a slow driver, you will manifest these traits in races. On the other hand, if you learn to see yourself as a winner and a competent driver, this too will manifest itself in performance. Don't worry if you did not picture yourself winning; I personally found this to be a difficult task at first. It may take some work to get to that point.

You may think this sounds a bit crazy, but begin your visualization process by getting into your racecar with your helmet and driver's gloves on. Let go of worries about looking or feeling stupid. (Although if you have a garage, that would be the ideal place to do this.) While getting into the racecar will enhance this exercise, you can also use mental imagery just about anywhere. It is helpful to find a quiet place though. Now close your eyes and take four deep breaths, inhaling and exhaling slowly. If you are not physically in the racecar, envision yourself in the car. Visualize your surroundings on the grid. Feel the weather, hear the sounds, inhale the smells – imagine everything as if you are there. Picture the workers while you drive the track. Since this is the qualifying session, don't focus much on the other cars on the track. Instead, spend time visualizing turning perfect laps in your head. Drive each lap with the perfect line and the least amount of braking needed. Feel the racecar and how it reacts to bumps on the track, when you brake and go around turns. Envision everything just the way it should be done. If you make a mistake while visualizing, go back, rewind, slow down the image in your mind, and do that part of the track over again. While doing this exercise, control your breathing. The qualifying session is now completed, and you drive back to your paddock spot. You are now ready for the race. Take a minute, open your eyes and relax.

Close your eyes again and take a few more deep breaths. Picture yourself on the grid again. And yes, you qualified first. As you did before, visualize all of your surroundings. The corner worker signals for you to enter the track and begin the warm-up lap. Picture the corner workers waving to you as you warm your tires and brakes. As you begin to approach the starting line, focus even harder, as you would in a race. Feel the anticipation as you watch for the green flag to be waived. Visualize a perfect race. Focus on hitting every apex and carrying the perfect amount of speed in every corner... Before you know it, this will transition over to when you drive on the track.

Mental imagery has no monetary cost – use it!

Having Self-confidence Matters!

You will find that some drivers try to "psych-out" other competitors with their false self-confidence.

During one of my races, a driver who qualified two cars behind approached me. The driver was someone I had heard about, and whom I had recognized as being pretty quick out on the track. He said that I had better watch out or I may end up adding another dent to his car. I looked over, and his car surely had many dings on it. As you might imagine, I was a bit annoyed with him. During the first lap he was successful in getting by me and a few other people. How does the old saying go? What comes around goes around. During the fourth lap I saw him and his car off in the grass. I later learned that his car had a mechanical issue, causing the car to cease running. I can't say I felt too bad for the guy. I had a pretty good laugh at his expense!

Instead of using this tactic, work at developing *real* inner confidence. It's a more sure-fire and stable option. The only thing you really have control over is yourself. Don't invest too much effort in trying to control the actions or reactions of other drivers. After you have truly developed self-confidence, you will be less likely to be affected by the actions of other drivers, and you will be better able to react to and adjust to unusual situations or track conditions.

Goal setting is a very effective way to build self-confidence. Develop short-term, realistic and attainable goals. Throughout your club racing career, you should be establishing goals and revisiting them. Setting measurable goals, achieving them, and establishing new goals, while recognizing your achievements, will prove to be beneficial.

Nothing builds confidence like success. Depending upon the clubs in your area, it might be worthwhile (and fun!) to race with a club where the competition is not as strong. This is not saying that the drivers are not talented, but often the racecars may not be built to their maximum potential. By doing well and running in the front of the pack with them, you will build your confidence.

In *Sacred Hoops: Spiritual Lessons of a Hardwood Warrior* (1995), former NBA coach of the Chicago Bulls and Los Angles Lakers Phil Jackson wrote:

> "In basketball – as in life – true joy comes from being fully present in each and every moment, not just when things are going your way. Of course, it's no accident that things are more likely to go your way when you stop worrying about whether you're going to win or lose and focus your full attention on what's happening right at this moment."

Relax and have fun! The results will take care of themselves.

Physical Aspects

Many racers in the club level underestimate the importance of physical conditioning. Auto racing demands the highest level of performance from you, the driver. Small errors causing only tenths-of-a-second setbacks can make the difference between winning and losing. Being in good physical shape does impact your driving abilities. Especially as you get further into the race itself, having worked on your cardiovascular endurance will pay off. There are reasons why professional racers have personal fitness trainers and place an emphasis on physical conditioning. You also need to make sure that you get plenty of sleep and drink plenty of water before the event.

What Are Other Things You Can Do?

- Obtain additional seat time. Prior to attending practice days, establish goals for yourself and identify areas that you want to focus on. Maybe you are having a difficult time with a particular turn? Obtain suggestions from other drivers, and test these new techniques.
- Seek additional coaching. It is not necessary to go to an expensive racing school to accomplish this. Talk with other

drivers, and possibly post a discussion on your favorite
racing thread to determine who might be able to assist you.
Approach another seasoned racer who is well-respected in
racing to see if he would be willing to provide you some
paid coaching at an open track day. Do remember that, just
because someone is an excellent driver, it does not mean
they will be an excellent coach. The person you seek should
typically be someone who drives a racecar in a different class.
Maybe even someone who drives in a different series. (No
one wants to give away all of their secrets to a fellow competitor.)

- Continue to study your in-car video. Pay attention to your
  driving techniques and to those of other people.

The Cheatn' Side of Town

I suppose it is just human nature for some people to cheat. When
you get to the point in your racing career where your next goal is to
start winning races, cheating can become tempting for some people. I
have heard many ways people attempt to rationalize cheating, such as,
"Everyone else is, so why shouldn't I?" When I personally say cheating
in this context, I am not referring to a missing washer bottle, horn or
other silly item. What I am talking about are "illegal" (against club
rules) modifications that the racer has done to the car that will improve
its performance. This is also different from pushing the rules and how
they can be interpreted. If you honestly feel that the way the rules are
written will legally allow you to perform a modification, then do it.

At one point, I was speaking with another seasoned racer about
cheating in club racing. During the conversation I mentioned that it
could not be very gratifying for me to win if I knew my car was bla-
tantly illegal. His response was, "Then obviously you have never won."
At that point he was correct, I had never won. After winning my first
race, I thought back to that statement, and I confidently knew how
wrong he was. Yes, it would have mattered. If I had not won through
my own skill as a driver, the victory surely won't have been so sweet.

While some people may get away with cheating for a while, it often
catches up to them. One gentleman was thought to have been cheating
for many races. At one of the races a formal protest was filed against
him, and his car was found to be illegal. He was disqualified from the

race, and he had points put on his license. For this racer, the "what goes around" came around. I could not help but chuckle while watching his car's engine blow-up in the next two subsequent events. Was it worth it for him to cheat?

Are You Ready to Spend Some Money?

Finally, we get to discuss modifications to your racecar! One of the first things you need to do is determine if your racecar has the potential to win in the club(s) you've chosen to race with as the car is currently classified. The key word here is *potential* to win. As previously mentioned, to be very successful, it takes a complete package consisting of a very good driver and a well-prepared car. Clubs have no guarantees that every car classified will be competitive. You will also learn that some clubs are better than others in classifying cars to ensure it has the potential of being competitive.

When it comes down to it, you choose the car you race. Even if your car is classed well, it still might be a better value to buy someone else's car, depending on what performance modifications have already been done to it. After reading this book, calculate how much it would cost you to develop the car. Then give thought to how much it would cost you to buy a well developed car. Determine the minimum amount you would accept for your racecar if you were to sell it – be realistic, and remember just how much Racecarious Depreciatous occurs (from The Racecar chapter). The last piece in this equation is to do the math. Write all of this information down, with specific allowances for each go-fast part or other goodie. If the car has good potential in the class, and if the math proves that you should develop your car, keep to the budget you just created, and move forward with developing the car. You also need to consider the amount of time and effort it will take to develop your car. As with the question "to buy or to build," there are similar pros and cons of moving forward with the development of your car.

There will always be a faster racecar no matter how much money and effort you put into yours.

There are some components that will generally yield more gains than others, regardless of the vehicle you are racing, such as better tires and a race built engine. There are also many items which will affect one type of car differently than another. For this reason, you will need to do some research on which modifications and parts will benefit your vehicle the most. Even with one particular modification, there are often several brands and variations of the part to choose from. Especially with the costs associated in developing the car, it is important that you take the time to research your options. The list below is categorized into three different, generalized priority levels – high, medium, and low. Again, this applies in general and may be different for the type of vehicle you race.

Tires: High

Having the right tires is very important when you are trying to whittle down your lap times. Although the initial cost to purchase the tires is typically within the general price range of the other tires you should have been using, there is an additonal financial price tag of using these faster tires. As a general rule, the faster tires often sacrifice longevity for improved handling. After transitioning into this "Moving On" phase, my tire budget doubled. Tire technology is ever changing – do your research on which is the current tire to have.

Race Engine Build: High

If you want to have a shot at winning races, it will be necessary to have a race engine built. How much horsepower will a built engine produce? There are many variables that will impact these figures, such as the vehicle's engine that is being built (some are more receptive to engine builds than others), how it is being built (including what the club allows you to do), the parts being used, etc. To give you an approximate idea, a good (yet legal) SCCA Improved Touring engine will gain approximately 15% - 20% of its stock horsepower. Again, this is a very rough calculation, and the performance gains are dependent upon what other modifications have been done to the car.

The prices to get your engine built (yes, you provide the engine that they will modify) will vary depending upon the builder, what you are having done, the condition of the engine you provide the builder, as well as other variables. To give you a rough idea, a well built engine complying with SCCA's Improved Touring rules would typically cost between $3,000 and $5,000. When shopping for your engine builder, determine if they have experience building engines for the clubs you race with. If they specialize in open-wheel formula racecar engines, you might want to seek another builder. Nothing says that someone who has not built an engine that complies with a specific club can't perform the build, but it does make things easier if they are already familiar with the applicable rules. It is your responsibility to ensure that the engine build be done within the club's rules. Get very specific information as to what will be done as part of the engine build process and what parts they will be using. Another question to ask is, "How will I receive the engine?" Will it be completely put together, including transmission, and ready for installation? Do they include resurfacing and balancing the flywheel into the engine build price? Determine any other costs (such as a new clutch) that you should figure into your budget. For example, during this race engine process, it would also be a good time to have a limited slip differential and racing clutch installed.

Once the engine build is completed, it will be necessary to install it. Ask how much the builder would charge to complete this for you. Another good option is for you to install the engine yourself. For me, personally, even just thinking about this process was stressful. Me, take the old engine out, then later install the new engine? Seriously? I looked into the engine bay and saw a mass of wires and other "things". I spoke with my engine builder, but he simply did not have the time to install the engine himself. He agreed to mate the transmission to the engine so it would be "ready to go" into the car. I couldn't help but think "Great, maybe I should have kept the stock engine in the car. At least I knew the car would run then." Looking back on things now, the process was very educational in that I learned that it is not rocket science, especially if you are the one to take the stock engine out. When taking the engine out of the car, I took many, many photos with a digital camera and labeled absolutely everything very clearly. While the process was extremely time consuming, it made the install much easier. After installing the new engine and getting the car started, I really felt proud. I also learned a lot about the car and myself during this process. Assuming the engine builder mates the transmission and other parts are assembled, it typically won't require many specialty tools, other than an engine hoist, to install the engine. When taking the engine out and installing the new one, consider borrowing or renting an engine hoist versus buying one.

Once the engine is installed, you will need to break the engine in. Recommendations on how to complete this process are conflicting. My suggestion is to speak with the engine builder, and break the engine in according to what they recommend.

Suspension and Handling Tuning: High

There are many books dedicated solely to racecar handling dynamics and there are many varied theories as to what is the best approach to tune the suspension. One critical piece of this subject is the adjusting of the racecar's alignment settings. To forewarn you, it may be necessary to make alignment adjustments for each specific track to tune the racecar properly. A good starting point is to use a probe-type pyrometer and tire pressure gauge to make initial adjustment settings. I purposely state a probe versus an infrared pyrometer because it more accurately measures tire temperatures. A basic probe-type pyrometer can be purchased for about $130. Using this tool and a sheet similar to the one shown in the appendix, measure the tire temperatures as well as the tire pressures. This will give you an idea of what adjustments will be necessary. Using a basic tuning theory, the tire temperatures should be consistent among the outside, middle and inner sections of the tire. What this indicates is that the entire surface of the tire is in contact with the track surface, providing the largest contact surface. If you are not able to obtain a near optimum alignment setting using the racecar's stock equipment, it may be necessary to modify it or purchase items such as camber plates to achieve the desired settings.

In addition to alignment tuning, if you have adjustable struts, it will be necessary to fine tune these settings, possibly testing different spring rates and rear sway bars, among other things.

Data Acquisition System: High

A data acquisition system is much more than just a go-fast part for your racecar. When used properly, it becomes an extremely valuable tool for driver improvement. So, what is a data acquisition system and how can it be used to improve your lap times?

This "black box" system stores a wide range of vehicle data for later analysis on a computer, although an in-car display can often be used to provide some instant feedback. Since data acquisition systems require use of a computer, the ideal situation is to have a notebook computer to bring to the track versus downloading the information at home after the event. (If your primary reason to own a notebook computer is to use it with a data acquisition system, it is not difficult to find a new one under $600. Used ones can be found for even less.) The data acquisition system can be used to improve driver performance as well as improve the racecar's performance. Most of us have gone through corners believing we are driving the fastest line, not lifting off the gas pedal, and braking as efficiently as possible. The challenge becomes how to truly measure this? Evaluating lap times can be used as a benchmark, but that only provides feedback on the entire lap and is difficult to determine where the gains or losses occurred. Making evaluations by the seat of your pants often provides inaccurate information. "I didn't lift at all through that corner." Are you sure? If you're like most of us, you have compared racing lines with friends and swear that one line is the fastest. With a data acquisition system, there's no need to continue guessing and making assumptions.

The data acquisition system I chose was the DL1 from Race Technology USA (www.Race-Technology.com). In addition to this system, there are others that will work similarly and provide useful data. The Race Technology system, as well as some other systems, utilize a GPS technology based logger augmented by internal dual axis accelerometers, which provides users accurate track maps, multiple sector times, true vehicle speed, and other analysis tools without the need of trackside beacons. The DL1 system costs just under $1,000 and includes vendor support. It is easy to use and set-up, and if some of your friends utilize the same system you can compare data with each other. When looking at various systems, it is also important to ensure that the software that comes with the system is effective and user friendly.

One potential way to reduce the cost of obtaining a data acquisition system is to share one with a friend. If your friend races in a group that will not be on the track at the same time as you, this could work very nicely. (The DL1 and some other systems can be moved from one car to another in just a couple of minutes.) Once you obtain a data acquisition system, it is important that you learn how to effectively use the information it collects, otherwise it just becomes an expensive lap timer. Some companies provide coaching services on how to better use the system, whether it is via the phone and e-mail, internet web conference or in-person. If you do not know someone who is very familiar with the data acquisition system you are using, I sincerely believe that obtaining coaching is money well spent. Fast Tech Limited, which is also a vendor of Race Technology products, provides various coaching services (www.FastTech-Limited.com) at a reasonable price.

Exhaust: High

The vehicle's stock exhaust can be very restrictive of the airflow. If you have not already, you should eliminate the catalytic converter and have a high flow exhaust installed using larger diameter exhaust piping. By doing this, you will allow greater exhaust flow and obtain performance gains. Bring your car to a well-respected exhaust shop and have them build a custom exhaust for your car. There are two different types of bends the exhaust shop can utilize when fabricating the exhaust. The first type, utilizing a "tube bender", is most common and produces the least expensive exhaust system. It bends the straight tube around a die. The down side of press bending is that the outside diameter of the tube in the middle of the bend will crinkle and cause airflow to become restricted and disturbed. The engine now has to use more of its horsepower to push the exhaust gas through the pipes, thus sacrificing performance. The second method of pipe bending is called mandrel bending. This style of bending utilizes a series of retractable and snug fitting, lubricated steel balls inside that section of pipe while being bent. This design keeps the pipe from shrinking or crinkling during the bending process, due to the steel balls inside the bend, thus providing the highest possible air flow. When you are looking for an exhaust shop, verify that they will be using mandrel bends. The cost of a custom exhaust varies, but for a very good quality exhaust, anticipate paying approximately $500.

Air Intake System: High

If the car has a stock air intake system, and especially if you have completed other exhaust work, this will be a worthwhile modification. If you can't get air into the engine fast enough, it really does not matter nearly as much how quickly it can exit. The typical cost is $170 – 200.

Limited Slip Differential: Medium

To better understand how a limited slip differential (LSD) can be advantageous, let's first look at how a standard differential works. When a vehicle using a standard differential has one wheel without contact to the ground and is powered by the engine (FWD vs. RWD), the contacting wheel will remain stationary, and the non-contacting wheel will rotate at twice its intended velocity. The result of this is no power being applied to the wheel on the ground. As in this example, the differential will supply the power to the wheel that is loaded with the least amount of resistance. In normal everyday driving, the likelihood of this situation occurring is very rare, or at least should be, except in slippery conditions. Even if it does briefly occur, losing ¼ second won't cause you to be late for work or be a safety concern. During a race, when cars are cornering close to their limits and drivers are looking to shave lap times down as much as possible, experiencing this issue costs valuable time. So how does a LSD solve this problem? This type of differential allows some difference in wheel rotation velocity, but does not allow the difference to increase beyond a pre-set amount. What the LSD essentially does is sense which wheel has the better grip and biases the power to that wheel without completely removing power from the other wheel. This translates into the car having more power to the ground in extreme cornering situations. Even if your vehicle comes stock equipped with a LSD, there are typically differences between units built for a sports car versus a racing application. Your vehicle and the tracks that you race on will impact how much of a benefit the LSD will yield.

There are two different types of mechanical LSDs available. One type is a geared torque-sensing version that uses planetary gears to sense the torque on the drive shafts. The geared torque LSDs typically won't wear like a clutch type could, but it is believed that the torque distribution characteristics can be less than ideal for racing purposes. The other type of LSD that I just referenced is the clutch type LSD. With this type of differential, clutch packs are installed which have varying degrees of force applied depending upon the differential wheel velocity. (Phantom Grip is a company that sells an LSD that somewhat emulates the clutch type using a spring block, but does not have clutches. I am not very partial to the Phantom Grip units for racing, but they do have a place outside of racing applications.)

Once you have determined which LSD you want to purchase, you also need to determine how it will be installed. Attempting to install an LSD would be very difficult for someone other than an experienced mechanic. My suggestion is to have the company where you purchased the LSD also install it if they offer that service.

Assuming the shop is not within easy driving distance from you, ship your transmission to them. It is an easier process than one might think. The first step is to get two boxes that the transmission will fit into. Trim one of the boxes down in size so it will fit into the other box. Completely drain the fluid out of the gearbox, then put a label on it identifying the model of the car and your name. All you need to do now is put a plastic bag around the transmission, put it into the box, and stuff the remainder of the box with newspapers or shipping Styrofoam peanuts. It is now ready to begin its journey. How can you ship the tranny? This surprised me a bit, but shipping companies such as UPS, FedEx Ground, DHL, and United States Postal Service will ship it at a reasonable cost. Shop around to determine which company offers the best price and service.

The other option would be to bring the LSD and stock transmission to a reputable transmission shop and have them complete the installation. One benefit of having the company which supplies the LSD unit complete the installation is that if there are any issues, they can't say it is because you had it installed incorrectly. In addition to having a company install the LSD, I recommend that you also have them rebuild your transmission.

Prices for the LSD range from $600 - $1,500 depending on the type of LSD and company you choose to purchase it from. For just the clutch type unit that I purchased, it cost me $700 for the LSD alone. When I had my LSD installed and tranny rebuilt, it cost me an additional $300 plus parts, for a total of $375 for the rebuild and installation. If your tranny is not in good shape, the cost to rebuild it will obviously be more but it is much better to know and take care of this now. Since you have the tranny off the car, now would be an opportune time to replace the clutch if that has not been done recently. A good quality racing clutch kit typically costs $300 - $375.

Race Exhaust Header: Medium

Although the header is a part of the exhaust system, this is considered to be a separate component. There are many different types of headers available from off-the-shelf units to dyno-tuned racing headers. For a decent header, anticipate paying approximately $400 - $600.

Blueprint Stock Fuel Injectors: Medium

People are often led to believe that it is necessary to purchase higher flow fuel injectors, but that is often not the case. In many cases, you can use your stock fuel injectors, but it might be worth having them "cleaned." When using your stock fuel injectors, especially in higher mileage cars, the injectors may not flow optimally anymore. By having a company such as RC Engineering (www.RCeng.com) blueprint your stock injectors, any contaminants that may impede fuel flow or degrade the fuel spray pattern will be removed. The approximate cost for this service is $30 per fuel injector.

Basic Engine Dyno Tuning: Medium

After you have a race engine built and installed, along with some of the other go-fast items listed, dyno-tuning can prove to be a valuable investment. I brought my car to the dyno shop with low expectations, thinking this process would at least provide me an idea of how powerful the engine was. I certainly was not expecting the results that the car gained simply from adjusting the fuel pressure and engine timing. My Improved Touring B Honda Prelude (110 stock HP at the crank) gained 6.5 maximum horsepower and 3.6 pounds of torque at the wheels. Even more important was how the horsepower and torque curves were modified throughout the RPM range. In my case, this certainly was well worth the $150 investment to have the shop tune the engine.

In order to have your engine properly dyno-tuned, it will be necessary to install an adjustable fuel pressure regulator. When I first purchased a fuel pressure regulator, I bought a very inexpensive unit that utilized a portion of the stock regulator. I soon returned the item and bought a better quality unit. I then went to a parts store (NAPA) and had them fabricate a fuel hose and adaptors for me to use when installing the fuel pressure gauge. If you are unable to locate a shop to do this, you can easily assembly the hose and adaptors yourself. But for the price I paid, it came out to about the same amount of money to have the shop do it for me the "right way." Before installing the fuel pressure regulator, install the fuel pressure gauge and determine what the current fuel pressure is. After installing the aftermarket fuel pressure regulator, set it to the amount that the stock fuel pressure regulator was and verify that the new set-up does not leak. If you don't do a baseline dyno run (with the stock fuel pressure and timing settings), you will never know what horsepower gains were made prior to tuning the car.

Some cars also have the ability of tuning the vehicle's ECU (engine control unit), using after market parts to better take advantage of the modifications you have completed on your racecar. The cost of these units ranges significantly and also requires time on a dyno to tune it.

Summary of Primary Costs:
Adjustable fuel pressure regulator: $170
Fuel Pressure Gauge: $20
Tap and die: $7
Drill bit: $6
Teflon tape for thread fittings: $1
Fuel hose and accessories for gauge: $16
or

NAPA assembled unit: $20

Light Weight Rims: Low

Depending on the weight of your current rims, you could benefit from purchasing some lighter weight rims. Reducing the racecar's overall weight is the first potential benefit. If you are having difficulties in getting close to the minimum allowable weight for your car's class, using rims that weigh four pounds less each can help. The other benefit is that using a lighter weight rim reduces the amount of unsprung weight. Unsprung weight is what is on the outboard end of the suspension – what is not being "sprung" by the suspension. This includes wheels, tires, brake components (rotors, calipers, drums), suspension arms, spindle, rear axle, and associated brake components. By reducing unsprung weight, you are reducing mass in motion. Less weight moving up and down means that the suspension can react more quickly to changing road surfaces and keep the tires planted on the ground better. This all equals slightly faster acceleration, traction, cornering traction, and overall better handling, to a degree.

When buying new rims, you should verify that they would work with the racecar's existing wheel studs. I bought some nice used lightweight rims, but when I went to see if they fit the car properly, I realized that the wheel studs were not long enough for these rims. For my car, the longer wheel studs cost another $50; then, of course, I needed the lug nuts that would fit, costing another $40. You also need to verify that the offset of the rim fits the car's needs. Of course, you want to buy the widest rims allowed by the club(s) you race with. There are many sources of lightweight rims, from used or new racing wheels, to used stock rims from various manufactures. The VW rims that I purchased weighed 11.5 pounds and were relatively inexpensive compared to other options. If you shop around, it is possible to find a good set of four used, lightweight wheels for $300 - $375. A set of new racing wheels often costs in excess of $800. Light weight rims will only get you so much of a performance gain. I don't recommend that you spend a significant amount of money to save a pound or two per rim; there are better ways to spend your money.

Air Dam and Splitter: Low

Does adding an air dam and splitter really help for the type of car you will be racing? I have spoken with many very experienced people on this subject and obtained differing opinions. One negative aspect of installing an air dam is that it is prone to damage if (when) a person makes an off-course excursion. If you decide to install an air dam and splitter, my recommendation is that you don't spend too much money on the modification.

Summary

Do all of these modifications seem a bit expensive? No one said that it was going to be cheap to develop the racecar, and the process is never-ending. There are many other go-fast options you can look into, such as changing the gearing on the car and numerous opportunities for dyno testing. To build a well-developed racecar, you will need to combine various parts and modifications in order to obtain the optimum package. For example, if you have a very well tuned exhaust and header, but don't have an air intake system to take advantage of it, the performance package suffers. You must also determine in what order various modifications should be completed. As an example, it does not make sense to bring the racecar to get it dyno-tuned before installing the race engine you just bought. Although you might not do all of the above items, usually you can still be very competitive if you focus very hard on improving your own racing skills. Give some serious thought to which items you choose to spend your money on. If it comes down to sacrificing your participation in races in order to buy several of these items, then they are probably not worth it.

11.

Is Sponsorship Possible?

People often believe that obtaining sponsorship at the club racing level is not possible, but that is not true. Before you start to seek potential sponsors, you need to establish realistic expectations and determine how much effort you are willing to put into it. While it is difficult to obtain cash sponsorships at the club racing level, sponsorship can come in many other forms. Here is a question that you need to give some thought to – why do you want to pursue sponsorships? Is it because you need financial sponsors to race at the club level? If the answer is yes, then you are better off getting another source of income to support your racing. If you are relying on sponsorship, you will create a lot of stress for yourself while trying to do something that should be fun. If it would be nice to have sponsors, but you are not financially dependent upon it, then great! Sponsorship can add to the enjoyment of racing if it is approached in the right manner. Seek sponsorships for the right reasons, and go into it with the right mindset.

Many people suggest that it would be better to take the time that you are planning to spend on your sponsorship efforts, and get a part-time job. The positive side of the part-time job is that it is guaranteed income, knowing that your efforts will result in a paycheck. Remember that sponsorship is also work to some degree and can become stressful at times. On the other hand, it can also be enjoyable and a great learning experience. Do you want to learn what the racing business (yes, I did say *business*) is really about? Beyond club racing, obtaining and retaining sponsors is extremely important in the racing industry. In professional racing, what do you think constitutes a successful racecar driver? Surely your driving skill and racing record is important, but you live and die by your ability to obtain sponsorship. You could be an extremely talented driver, but if you can't bring money to the team, it will be very difficult to succeed. On the other hand, a person could be a good driver, perhaps not quite as talented, but have a strong ability to obtain sponsors. That person will find things much easier. Honestly, an entire book could be devoted just to the sponsorship topic. This chapter discusses the basics of racing sponsorship at the club level and will provide you with enough knowledge to begin your own sponsorship campaign. You should also understand that there are differences in obtaining and maintaining sponsors between the club racing level and professional levels.

Why would a business want to become your sponsor? This is a question that you need to give thought to and incorporate it into your sponsorship plan. Sponsoring your "racing team" is a marketing opportunity for a business. Seek out businesses that would most benefit from what you can provide them. Again, set realistic expectations and goals. When approaching a potential sponsor, focus on what you can do for them, not what they can do for you. If you use the opposite approach, you will be walking out the door empty-handed quite frequently. There are reasons why a business can benefit from sponsoring your race team, and it is your job to point these reasons out to them. To give you a starting point, I have listed a few potential benefits for sponsors below.

- Hopefully the major benefit to the company is you! Try to think of ways you might be able to help promote their business. Talk the business up.
- Publicity for the business. While there are not typically a significant number of fans at club races, there are other drivers, corner workers, friends, and family in attendance.
- Employee morale. It can be fun for a business to be involved in a race team.
- Potential tax write-off. If you own a business, this may also be an excellent opportunity for you! When discussing this with a potential sponsor, be very careful. I strongly suggest that anytime this is mentioned, you state it as a *potential* tax benefit, and recommend that they consult a tax advisor.
- The dream of wanting to be racecar driver. For those people who have always dreamed about racing themselves, this will allow them to become involved in racing through you.

- Bragging rights. The business owner can brag to their friends that they sponsor a race team.

A common question asked in club racing is: Do you need to be a winning driver to obtain sponsors? I personally found the answer to this question to be very surprising – the answer is no! It is even possible to obtain sponsors before you begin your first racing season, even before you have a racing license. So what does it take? The first and most important step is to get out there. Sounds simple enough, but this step is one of the hardest parts in the process. Approach people with a big smile and a well thought out sponsorship proposal. The goal during this first visit should be to "sell" the business owner or manager into wanting to talk with you a bit further about the sponsorship opportunity when they have some time, or if you are really lucky, right then. Respect the fact that they are trying to operate a business, and that their time is usually very limited. You also need to be prepared to be rejected many times before you finally land a sponsor. Don't take it personally! Pursuing sponsorships is very similar to many other types of sales, and you need to treat it that way. I know, I know. I just said the evil "sales" word. Think of it this way, you are selling yourself and something that you are very passionate about. Really, what do you have to lose, other than hearing the words "no thanks"? I also realize that it is easier said than done, but it is the attitude you need to have.

When speaking with potential sponsors, make sure that you spend your efforts talking with a decision maker, or at least with someone who has close contact with the decision maker of that business. Otherwise it is simply a waste of your time. It only takes one or two companies to make sponsorship worthwhile. Keep plugging away; it will come. The key is persistence, persistence and guess what? Persistence. One tool I found useful is to create a sponsorship package to provide potential sponsors. Additional information about sponsorship proposals is discussed later in this chapter. Just because you drop off an impressive sponsorship package, don't expect the business to be calling you. It often takes several follow-up calls before actually obtaining a sponsor. Sponsorship is a bit like dating. For the longest time you just can't seem to even buy a date (well, in most states anyway), and then finally you have a significant other. Now, all of a sudden you have a ton of girls (or guys) wanting you! It is ironic how it works that way, but let's say it has to do with an increased confidence level. This same theory often applies to finding sponsorships.

When I started attending club races, I walked around the paddock and looked at all of the amazing racecars with their sponsors' names on the cars. I became curious about how they obtained their sponsors and what the race team received from them. During this process, I learned that many racers are their own sponsors. What I mean by this is that the person driving the car owns his own business, or has a friend or relative who is a business owner that sponsors the race team. It may be an overly-quoted phrase, but it is so true: "It's not what you know, but who you know." So, who do you know? Do you have a family member or friend who owns a business? Possibly a friend of a friend? Or even better yet, do you own your own business? Think of all the businesses you have built some type of relationship. Use all of your potential resources, and don't be afraid to ask. Using networking to obtain sponsorships is extremely important. The squeaky wheel bearing gets the grease. By all means, I am not suggesting that you ask for a handout from a friend or relative; truly approach this as a sponsorship relationship.

As previously mentioned, sponsorship can come in many different forms. The first thing that comes to mind when thinking sponsorship is cash. Quite honestly, this form of sponsorship is very difficult to obtain at the club racing level, but there are other forms of sponsorship that will be as good as cash to you. Take time to prepare a list of the types of businesses you will approach, and give consideration to the various forms of sponsorship they could provide you. What are a few types of businesses that you may want to consider approaching? To provide you a very basic starting point, the following are types of places to consider:

- Auto body Shops: They might be willing to paint your racecar, repair damage incurred during races, etc.
- Used car dealerships: Typically when used car dealerships purchase their used cars, they purchase them in "lots". These lots (or packages) of cars often have vehicles that the dealership does not want to sell at their dealership. While these vehicles don't represent much value to the dealership, they can be very valuable to you. Do you need an inexpensive tow vehicle? What about a parts car? What about a fixer upper?

(Unfortunately, due to insurance reasons, it is usually very difficult to get a business to loan you a vehicle to use for towing purposes.)

- Garages: Do you currently need any mechanical work done on the car? Or maybe they would be willing to provide you future help with the car. Another possibility is for the garage to mount your race tires and do other basic maintenance for you.
- Salvage yards: This is a great source for used parts, which you will definitely need!
- Performance muffler shops: They could provide you with a racing exhaust system. If they are not willing to sponsor the entire cost, approach them with another option: Maybe they would be willing to provide you with the work at no cost and charge you only their cost for materials.
- Need a place to store your vehicle? Try a self-storage business. A few other great options are landscaping businesses (they all have places to store their equipment) and farms (you may be able to use some of their barn space).
- Auto parts stores: It may be tough to get parts for free, but often times it is possible to get them at a discounted rate. Parts stores usually have "regular consumer" rates as well as "contractor" rates. It is not unheard of for a parts store to offer racers the contractor rates, or even possibly parts at cost.
- Sign shop: The business could provide the vinyl lettering for your car, including other sponsor's basic lettering.

Be creative with your efforts! You are only limited by your imagination. The company does not even have to provide something directly related to racing. In fact, it is usually difficult to get a business that is directly related to racing to sponsor a race team. The reason is that the majority of their client base are racecar drivers; therefore, if they were to provide one racer support, but not others, it could upset their other customers. When giving thought to what companies could help with things that are unrelated to racing, think about how the sponsor could save you money in other areas of your daily life, thereby enabling you to put more towards racing. What things could possibly save you money? For example, do you have any pets? Sounds like a strange question, but when you go away for vacations, do you need to kennel them? Approach a kennel to sponsor you in return for taking care of your pets. Another reason why these forms of sponsorship are an easier sell is because they do not cost the business any out-of-hand cash.

When Should You Approach Prospective Sponsors?

Ideally, you will approach prospective sponsors when he is creating his upcoming year's budget, including marketing expenditures. The timing of this would be approximately three months prior to their fiscal year end. Many businesses utilize a fiscal year beginning July 1st, while others begin their fiscal year January 1st. Although it is much easier to postpone beginning your sponsorship search to fit into this schedule, don't procrastinate – begin now. While timing certainly is important, many times the decision does not hinge upon the company's budget, but the general attitude of the business owner and current financial outlook of the company. Since most businesses are not looking to provide cash sponsorship, the budget timing is not as important as it would be otherwise. The worst that happens is that the business owner will ask you to come back in a few months when he starts preparing his annual budget. The great thing is that you have now placed the sponsorship idea in his head.

Sponsorship Proposals

One effective tool you can utilize in the hunt for sponsors is a basic proposal. Keep the proposal relatively short and concise; otherwise, the chance of the prospective sponsor reading it will be very minimal. To keep your costs down, don't simply go around and haphazardly pass out your proposals. I have even heard of people doing mass mailings to companies with their proposals. This is a waste of time and money. As mentioned above, do some research on the companies you want to target, and visit them in person, if at all possible. Approach the business with something even as simple as....

> Hi, my name is _____. Is the owner of the business available? (If not, ask when the best time for you to come back might be.) I wanted to stop by and introduce myself to you. I race a (car type) with (car club) and would be interested in discussing how we might be able to help each other. Could I leave

you some information about this opportunity? (Provide the person the sponsorship proposal.) Thank you for your time.

Don't wait for them to call you. In about four or five days, call the person you provided the proposal to, and ask if it might be possible for you to stop by at some point that is convenient to talk a bit more. Up until this point, your goal is not to sell the person on a sponsorship partnership – just focus on selling a time to talk with him further. Then work on selling him on the sponsorship.

The Appendix of this book includes a sample proposal that I created and utilized. Please feel free to use it as a starting template.

What To Do Now That You Have a Sponsor

Which is more intimidating, trying to get the sponsor, or determining what to do now that you actually have one? Try not to feel overwhelmed. It is not expected that you spend a significant amount of money wining and dining your sponsors, although you absolutely must show your appreciation and make an effort to bring the company business. Sure, you will put the company's name on the car, but there is much more to it than just that.

As a minimum, get some of the company's business cards to have on hand at all times. Does this mean that you need to spend time walking around handing them out? No, but it certainly looks good that you have them readily available for people to take. In addition to bringing the business cards to the track with you, try to have a few with you at all times. Put a few in your wallet or pocketbook. Keep in mind that the best thing you can do for your sponsor is to attract more business for them.

As discussed throughout this book, you need to use a little creativity. If the company does not already have a brochure, consider creating a brochure or flyer, and make it available at the track. Send the sponsor a well-written letter, including a schedule and update on your season. Have some basic tee shirts or hats made with your sponsors' name on it, and give a few to your sponsors. Proudly wear them while at the track.

During the racing season, ask your sponsors to come to the track to watch some of your events. I do realize that it can be scary to have your sponsor come to an event when you are just beginning, but try to just think of them as some friends who are coming to watch you race. While they are at the track, make sure you pay attention to them and introduce them to your crew, other racers, and anyone else you know. Of course, be sure to mention their company name and what their business does. A plastic table, tablecloth, some cheese, cookies, and beer can go a long way. Be aware that most clubs limit the number of people you can add to your crew. Typically a race team's crew is limited to three or four people total per event. Many times clubs/tracks charge entrance fees to spectators who are not a part of a team's crew. The reason why I mention this is that you don't want to start offering tickets to all of their employees for the races. You may want to approach the club you race with to determine if they could provide some additional tickets for your sponsors to use.

The main thing is to show your sponsors that they are important, and that you took the time to put effort into their sponsorship. Whether it is during the racing season or off-season, occasionally visit your sponsor, even if it means stopping by to quickly to say hello. Don't worry if they don't spend time talking with you, as they do have a business to run. By making these visits, it will show your sponsors that you are thinking about them, which will help strengthen your relationship.

For a "big" sponsor (and you need to define this one), you may consider allowing them to use your car in a high performance driving event. This does not have to include your paying for the event, but allow them to use your car with some practice tires. Assuming the person drives in a novice group, they will be significantly restricted as to how fast they can go and will only be able to pass on straights. Since you should be the person instructing them (yet again adding to the experience), you control how hard they push the car. Talk about leaving a great impression on the business owner!

At the end of the season, give them a framed picture of your car with a thank-you card. Bring them a nice bottle of wine or some beer. Again, it is not all about how much you spend, but rather you're showing that you are putting effort into the relationship. Remember to put things in perspective. If things don't go well with your sponsor, what is the worst that happens? They don't sponsor you next year. If you truly put effort into showing your appreciation, you have absolutely nothing to be ashamed about.

As I continue to say throughout this book, have fun with this! If you are doing it properly, you have very little to lose and much to benefit and learn from through the sponsorship process. Good luck!

Appendix A:

The Costs of Racing

In order to control racing costs, it is necessary to take some time to research and shop around. When purchasing many items, used items that are still in good condition is a very good option. Look at eBay, racing web sites, and other various places. When buying new items, again, take the time to shop around. It is amazing to look at the varying prices a person could pay for even very basic items. To help control your expenditures, define the various items that you need versus items you want. Do you need a 260 piece tool set? Do you need a racing jack? Do you need a race built engine? You get the point.

Being creative with your efforts can also go a long way in reducing your racing budget.

Consider selling your used tires if they are still in decent shape (not corded or flat spotted) on eBay targeting autocrossers. Yes, I have done this and am surprised at the amount of money people will pay for used racing tires.

Tire mounting: some racing tire manufactures will mount tires for free or at a discounted rate if you go to one of their distributorship locations. Some repair and tire shops owned by people who also race give other racers a price break. Ask around if someone in your area has any leads.

When looking at costs, don't ignore the smaller ticket items that you will be purchasing. Windshield cleaner, brake fluid, paper towels, wires, zip ties, bolts, beer for you and your crew all add up. It is very easy to make a quick trip to the home improvement store and spend $50 or more on these types of small ticket items.

Should you put a dollar figure on your time? My opinion is no. It is not that your time isn't valuable, it is that you are spending your time on a hobby that you enjoy. Racing did not choose you, you chose to race. When you are pushing a car to its limits and many times beyond, things will happen. Racing is a time consuming sport between general maintenance, repairs, studying, and the events themselves. I have heard the argument that people should associate $10 (as a minimum) for each hour they spend working on the racecar. While you do want to budget your time, the idea of associating a monetary amount per hour seems a bit silly. How much did sitting down watching television cost you? If you were to play basketball, would you associate an hourly figure shooting around? Think about all of the other activities you do – each has an associated trade off. If you have a job where you have the ability to earn additional money by working a few extra hours, then it makes sense to evaluate how long a project would take you to complete versus having someone else complete the work. But then again, that somewhat defeats the purpose. Hopefully time will be spent on your racing hobby because you enjoy it.

Beep, Beep, Beep
Warning!

The following can lead to severe headaches and heartburn. Proceed with extreme caution. Having a strong beverage may be useful. The positive news is that it is not necessary to purchase all of these items at once. For example, plan on doing HPDEs for the first year, then plan on racing during the second year. This will spread many of the costs over time. (Listed prices do not include possible sales tax or shipping costs.)

Personal Safety Equipment Costs

Driver's suit: $240
Fire retardant underwear (top and bottom): $90 total
Fire retardant socks: $15
Fire retardant racing gloves: $40
Racing shoes: $40
Helmet (Snell SA rated): $250

Racecar Costs

Buy a Pre-built Racecar: $3,000 to the sky is the limit
Summary of Primary Costs to Build a Racecar:
Donor car*: Estimated $1,000
Custom-made roll cage: $1,200 - $1700
Roll bar padding: $15 - $20
Window net and mounting hardware: $35
Suspension: $900 - $1,500
Glass sunroof replacement: $59
Racing seat: $250
Racing harness and mounting bolts: $88
Kill Switch and related accessories: $66
Racing brake pads for the front (one set): $135 - $150
OEM style brake pads for the rear: $35
Brake fluid: $10 - $15
Brake ducts: $65
Engine oil (4 quarts): $20
Transmission oil (OEM): $12
Fire extinguisher: $40
Transponder: $300 - $335
Wink mirror: $20
Steel rims (4): $150
Corner weighting: 12 pack of beer to a fellow racer or $90 - $150 to have a shop complete it.
Alignment: Another 12 pack of beer or $90 - $150 to have a shop complete it.
Paint the interior and roll bar: $104
Tow hooks: $20
Anti-sway bar bushings: $10
Vinyl numbers and class lettering: $40
Club decals: $18
Factory shop manual: $60 - $100
Fuel port: $15

Does looking at these costs make you think more about buying a pre-built racecar? In addition to these costs, other seemingly minor costs will be incurred (such as wires, tape, cleaning products). The above budget also assumes that you won't be painting the exterior of the racecar.

* The donor car price can have a significant range depending on the car you choose to purchase. It is very possible to purchase a used car for approximately $600, but it also very easy to spend much more money. Also, budget for any necessary maintenance and repairs for the donor car.

Tool Costs

Before you start getting stressed out about the below tool prices, this list assumes that you do not currently have any tools. The majority of these items were priced using new Craftsman tools that were not on sale. The majority of the tools are better than what I have been using for several years now. As one example, the 53 piece tool set is a much nicer set than what I've used for several years. Fortunately there is good news with these items. It is not necessary for you to run out and purchase all of these items at once, and after you have the tools, you shouldn't need to replace them often. Many tool manufactures even have a lifetime guarantee where the company will replace them without any questions.

Tool box: $50
Safety glasses: $12
Painter's mask: $10 - $30
Box of 50 disposable latex gloves: $4
Metric and SAE tool sets: 53 piece $30; 117 piece $80
Inexpensive torque wrench: $10
Wire stripper: $20
Spark plug gap tool: $5
Flashlight: $20
Mechanics gloves: $25
Jack (an inexpensive one will suffice): $30
Jack stands (2): $20
Tire pressure gauge: $34
Drill: $20
Drill bits: $12
Set of metal files: $20
Set of pliers: $15
Tin shears: $12
Screwdriver set: $30

Set of adjustable wrenches: $30
Breaker bar: $25
Iron pipe (24" long, 1" diameter): $5
Large rubber hammer: $15
Metal hammer: $20
Large metal hammer (my favorite tool!): $22
Pry bar: $15
Ball bearing fork: $10
Jumper cables: $10
Home-built brake bleeder tool: $10

If you elect to build your racecar, there are a few additional tools that you will need. For example, if you have a sunroof and need to replace the skin thus possibly requiring a jigsaw ($30), blades ($10), rivet gun ($15) and rivets. When stripping the interior, you will also need a chisel ($10).

Annual Racing Budget

Acquiring a racecar is only one piece of your racing budget. As part of creating your budget, you also need to take into consideration the other costs associated with racing. Items such as clutches, wheel bearings, and axles, in addition to many other items may need to be replaced from time to time. As stated throughout the book, there are several factors that will impact your annual racing budget. A few of these items are as follows:

- The car you are racing – how hard is it on equipment including tires? My car is very hard on the front tires. A friend of mine who drives a Toyota MR2 can get at least twice as much use on the same tires as my car.
- Different tracks will impact wear on tires and brakes differently.
- The tires you are using. For example, the "fast" tires last me approximately three race weekends compared to tires that sacrifice some speed for longevity, which last approximately six race weekends.

While there are many expenses that you don't have control over, there are also many that you do. In the beginning of your racing career in particular, make your decisions based upon what will provide you the most racing and seat time. In order to give you a very basic idea, I have included a general summary of my racing costs during a "typical" season. This budget was based upon participation in six races and instructing at four high performance driving events. When you do your first year's budget, don't forget to also include the two competition licensing schools.

The car I drive is front-wheel-drive, 110 stock horsepower, and weighs approximately 2,500 pounds.

Sample Summary of Primary Costs:
SCCA membership fees:
    Membership dues: $60
    Regular competition license: $75
    Regional dues: $20
Annual tech inspection: budget $20
Racing event entry fees (6 races)*: $1,500
High performance driving event entry fees
    (instruct at 4 events): $0
Tires:
    Toyo RA-1 (6 shaved 205/60/13): $714
    Shipping: $54
    Mounting and balancing: $90
Rotors:
    Front (replaced once every 1 ½ years): $59
    Rear (replaced every 2 years): $22
Gas for racecar (races and HPDEs)**: $494
Engine oil (changed twice a year): $40
Oil filters (2 per year): $12
Racing brake fluid (flushed twice a year): $24
Fuel filter (replaced once every 2 years): $7
Spark plugs (replaced once every two years): $15
Windshield wipers (replaced once every two years): $12
Transmission fluid (replaced once a year): $20
Gas for the tow vehicle***:
    Lime Rock Park, CT (7 events): $150
    Watkins Glen, NY (1 event): $134
    New Hampshire International Speedway, NH
    (2 events): $143

Hotel rooms: not applicable (we camp)
Lunch: we spend no more money than otherwise to eat lunch
Dinner: included at the worker appreciation party
    Total: $3,665

A 6 event season keeps me very busy! This is especially true in the climate I live (New England) where there are less than 7 ½ months for racing. As stated throughout the book, the amount of money various people can budget for racing will vary dramatically. The above-stated costs will also vary depending on the club and region racing with, tire budget, proximity of the track(s), and so forth. You also need to budget for repairs that may be necessary.

For items noted above that are replaced in a time frame greater than one year, the costs shown are the amortized amount per year.

   * Or 4 races and 2 competition licensing schools at an average cost of $250

   ** 13 gallons x $3.80 per gallon x 10 events

   *** 15 mpg for the truck when towing; $3.30 per gallon (87 octane) = $0.22 per mile

Appendix B

Tire Pyrometer Sheet

Optimum tire temperature range manufacture recommends is:
_____

Recommended hot tire pressure range: _____
(Take tire temperatures without doing a cool-off lap.)
Camber:
Camber is good when the outside and inside temps are close.
If inside temp too high / outside too low, reduce the negative camber.
If inside temp too low / outside too high, increase negative camber.
Tire Pressures:
The middle tire temp should be approximately equal to the average of the outside and inside temps.
If too hot in the middle, lower the tire pressure.
If too cold in the middle, increase the tire pressure.

Front Left Tire Temps:

_____   _____   _____

Outside   Inside

Tire Pressure: _____

Front Right Tire Temps:

_____   _____   _____

Inside   Outside

Tire Pressure: _____

Rear Left Tire Temps:

_____   _____   _____

Outside   Inside

Tire Pressure: _____

Rear Right Tire Temps:

_____   _____   _____

Inside   Outside

Tire Pressure: _____

Appendix C

Sample Sponsorship Proposal

How This Sponsorship Will Benefit You and Your Business

A racecar sponsorship is more than just a rolling billboard. Sure, you will have your company's name on the car but there are many other valuable benefits.

- You get a driver who can help network and promote your business.
- Provide exposure for your business.
- Possible tax write-offs.
- Can be utilized to improve employee morale – it will definitely be fun for you and your employees to become involved in. You are welcome to get as involved with the racing team as you would like.

(Nice picture of the racecar)
What could I do for you to make this relationship worthwhile?
I would be more than happy to discuss any ideas you may have.

Your Name
Your Phone Number
Your e-mail Address

Common Myths About Motorsports Sponsorships:

Myth 1 - Providing sponsorship is simply too expensive. **Not true!** You determine how you would like to provide assistance to the race team – there are many different forms of sponsorship and it does not have to include financial support.

Myth 2 - All that you receive in return for sponsoring the team is your company's name on the car. As briefly stated on the front page, there are many other benefits you will receive.

How can motorsports sponsorship benefit your business?

Motorsports sponsorship can increase name awareness through visibility in the community, improve revenue, and employee morale. Of course, an added benefit is the potential tax break / advertising write-off you may be able to obtain for your business.

Have you ever passed a trailer carrying a racecar on the road? Let me ask you, did it catch your eye? The attention received while transporting the racecar to races is tremendous. Maybe we could park the car in front of your store? It will definitely draw attention. You'll find customers coming in and asking about the racecar.

Use the opportunity as a public relations vehicle by displaying the racing team picture on the wall of the office or store.

Racing sponsorship improves the loyalty of a company's employees. Think of simple things such as a polo shirt with the race team name and your company's logo on it. Racing events can be a very fun family outing - employees and their children would really appreciate a day at the track. Another incentive that can be used to build a company's morale is to allow an employee(s) to work on the car preparation. Obviously this will apply more if you are an automotive shop or related business.

Even if you personally have no interest in racing, you can still take advantage of the promotional advantage it can provide your business. Racing events can be a great environment for the prospective client or existing customer who happens to be a race fan. Again, use the opportunity to be creative and differentiate your company from other companies in your market. There is no doubt that more exposure in the community will translate into a sale down the road.

A racing sponsorship is more than just a rolling billboard...

You also get a driver who can help you network and promote your business. A driver's performance can be evaluated in several different areas. Is the driver a person you want representing and selling your company? What is the driver willing to do for you? Would you feel comfortable going to an event with your employees and prospective customers? How would the driver treat you?

I realize the importance of supporting my sponsors through many different methods and am always willing to discuss various ways that we can make this relationship even more beneficial to you.

What types of sponsorship opportunities are there?

There are many different ways you can provide sponsorship. Sometimes it just takes a little creativity. Of course there is always monetary support. You could also become a product sponsor by providing items needed for the racing season. Often times sponsors will provide racers with unique types of sponsorship that have no direct correlation to racing itself, but allow funds that would normally be spent on other products or services to be used for the race team. I would be more than happy to discuss *any* ideas you may have.

Additional Benefits Sponsors Will Receive

Your company's name will be placed on the racecar and may also include contact information such as your e-mail address, phone number, location, etc. You can also use this space for special promotional advertisements or as a reward to your suppliers or customers. The size of the sign will coincide with the value of support given. It is also possible to obtain in-car racing video with your company's name displayed on the car's dash. I would be more than happy to provide you with these videos for you to use for promotional purposes or simply for you to watch for fun. You will also receive SCCA race tickets and pit passes so you or others can attend races. Anyone interested in becoming more involved in racing is also welcome to become a part of the "race crew" for any of the events.

Basic signage to appear on the racecar will be provided at no charge. This includes all letters and numbers for your signs. If you are interested in incorporating pictures, logos or other advertising signage, it will be necessary to discuss how this will be provided.

What is SCCA road racing?

Road racing is conducted on paved roadways / tracks that utilize both left and right turns that form a track. Some professional examples of road racing leagues are the Indy Racing League, CART and Formula One. One of the clubs I race with is called the Sports Car Club of America (SCCA). The SCCA is a 55,000 member non-profit organization featuring the most active membership participation organization in motorsports today. There are several regions that make-up the SCCA. The New England Region (NER) has been the fastest growing region in the SCCA for the past six years and consists of over 3,100 members. The foundation of the SCCA remains its Club Racing program. The club racing program is very successful in grooming top-notch, world-class drivers and race officials.

The track that I race at most often is Lime Rock Park located in Lakeville CT.

The Racecar

The car is a 1987 Honda Prelude si and races within SCCA's Improved Touring B class.

Many fans, for obvious reasons, can easily associate with the vehicles in the Improved Touring class. It is this type of association of car styles that makes NASCAR so successful. While it is often difficult to picture yourself driving a Formula One car, it is easy to dream of racing a "regular" streetcar. To learn more about the SCCA, visit their web site at www.scca.org. To learn more about the New England Region of the SCCA, visit www.ner.org.

Please feel free to contact me to further discuss potential sponsorship opportunities and to learn more about its many benefits to you.

I would welcome the opportunity to meet with you in person to further discuss the benefits this relationship will provide you. Thank you for your consideration!

Your Name
Your Phone Number
Your e-mail Address

Appendix D

Racing Related References

*Don't forget to visit www.GoAheadTakeTheWheel.com
for racing videos, pictures, and more*

SCCA and NASA websites:

www.SCCA.org
www.NASAProRacing.com

Favorite Racing Chat Forums:

www.Honda-Tech.com
(Visit the Road Racing / Autocross section; it is not Honda specific)
www.ImprovedTouring.com
www.NASAforums.com
www.SCCAforums.com

Additional Suggested Periodicals:

Speed Secrets (the series of books)
The book *Going Faster*
Grassroots Motorsports Magazine
(www.GrassrootsMotorsports.com)

Racing Related Business References:

The following represent companies that I and many other racers have been pleased with both from a product and customer service perspective. Please keep in mind that there are numerous automotive businesses and this only represents a few of my recommendations.

Kessler Engineering
Improved Touring, Spec Miata and Nissan Specialists

From turn-key racecars, quality built and super fast engines,
and roll cages to general race preparation
www.KesslerEngineering.com

Koni North America
Winningest shock absorber manufacturer
in the history of motorsports

Adjustable shock absorbers & suspension kits
for street and race cars
(859) 586-4100
www.Koni-NA.com
www.KoniRacing.com

Race Technology USA
U.S. distributor of Race Technology products
including the DL1 data acquisition system
804-358-7289
www.Race-Technology.com

Fast Tech Limited
Retailer of Race Technology products including
the DL1 data acquisition system, and provides
various forms of coaching on how to effectively
utilize data acquisition systems.
614-216-9552
www.FastTechLimited.com

Carbotech Performance Brakes
Racing and high performance pads, shoes and rotors

Manufactures pads/shoes for virtually any vehicle
877-899-5024
www.CarbotechEng.com

Levine Auto & Truck Parts
Is it time to paint or repair your car?

Retailer of auto body supplies, paint, & much more
Shipping Nationwide
800-394-9012
www.LevineAutoParts.com

Chase Cam
Your Source for Video at Speed

Complete video systems, cameras, mounts
and other video accessories
619-583-4193
www.ChaseCam.com

Phil's Tire Service
Toyo, Hoosier, Hankook, Goodyear and Kumho race tires
as well as many other brands of street and track tires

In addition to shipping tires nationwide, Phil's Tire Service
provides trackside support for many of the Northeast racing events
845-429-8943
www.PhilsTireService.com

Appalachian Tire
Hoosier, Hankook and Toyo race tires
865-681-6622
www.RaceTire.com

Raxles
Your source for axles and CV joints
800-257-8192
888-257-8192
www.raxles.com

Bishop Motor Sports, LLC
Your source for all of your automotive performance
needs including suspensions, intakes, exhaust systems,
dyno tuning, corner weighting, and race alignments

www.BishopMotorsports.com
860-269-7821

Bildon Motorsport
Volkswagen Racing Equipment
www.Bildon.com

Shine Racing Service
VW, Audi specialists
For all of your racing and street needs
508-660-7974
www.srsvw.com

OPM Autosports
Honda – Acura – Mazda
Improved Touring and Production
Spec Miata
Parts, Service & Rentals
770-886-8199
www.opmautosports.com

RC Engineering
High performance & racing fuel injectors
Injector cleaning, balancing & blueprinting
310-320-2277
www.RCeng.com

Racer's Edge
Providing suspension, brakes, drivetrain, safety and
everything in between, from parts to turn key race
cars, we can help!
865-675-8285
www.RacersEdge-inc.com

Isaac, LLC
Head and neck restraints
www.IsaacDirect.com

Information about various head and neck
restraints can be found at: www.headrestraint.org

Mather Racewear
"Racewear for the Car and You"
Custom vinyl lettering, shirts and hats
www.MatherGraphics.com

FuelPorts.com
A great source for fuel test ports
fuelport@hotmail.com
www.FuelPorts.com

Additional Racing Businesses:

OG Racing
Source for racing equipment
supplies and safety gear
800-934-9112
www.ogracing.com

Driving Impressions
Source for racing equipment
supplies and safety gear
800-275-4667
www.teamdi.com

CDOC
Source for racing equipment
supplies and safety gear
800-915-2362
www.CDOC.com

Advanced Autosports
Various racing supplies; this company
has a strong focus on Spec Miatas
(I was really intrigued with their "spec
Miata in a box")
608-313-1230
www.Advanced-Autosports.com

I/O Port Racing Supplies
Auto racing safety equipment
orders: 800-949-5712
support: 925-254-7223
www.ioportracing.com

SoloRacer.com
Helmets, seats, harness belts and more
330-940-3249
www.SoloRacer.com

Apex Performance
Various racing supplies & safety equipment
866-505-2739
www.ApexPerformance.net

Solo Performance
Racing parts & equipment
877-614-SOLO
www.SoloPerformance.com

Solo Time
Racing parts & equipment
www.SoloTime.com

AWDirect
Trailer supplies, fire extinguishers
800-243-3194
www.awdirect.com

eBaymotors
eBay
Buy and sell various racing related
items

AMB
Timing transponders
(Check with your club & region
to determine if they sell the
transponders as part of a group buy)
Or www.AMB-it.com

Track Day Motorsports
Porsche Accessories
Safety gear & other equipment
440.725.9244
www.TrackDayMotorsports.com

Pegasus Auto Racing Supplies
Various racing supplies
800-688-6946
www.PegasusAutoRacing.com

Online Metals
Various metals including sheet metal
(Metal source for sunroof replacement
skin)
900-704-2175
www.onlinemetals.com

Racer Parts Wholesale
Racing parts & equipment
800-397-7815
www.racerpartswholesale.com

Racer Wholesale
Racing safety equipment
orders: 1-800-866-RACE
support: 800-397-7811
www.racerwholesale.com

Summit Racing
Performance racing parts
800-230-3030
www.summitracing.com

MazdaSpeed
Discounted Mazda Parts
(for racecars only)
800-435-2508
www.MazdaMotorsports.com

JC Whitney
Tools and other automotive supplies
www.JCWhitney.com

Craftsman Tools
www.sears.com
800-377-7414
Or got to a Sears store near you

Northern Tool & Equipment Co.
800-533-5545
www.northerntool.com

Harbor Freight Tools
800-423-2567
www.harborfreight.com

Bibliography

Lopez, Carl. *Going Faster.* Cambridge, MA: Bentley Publishers, 1997, 2001.

Jackson, Phil, Hugh Delehanty and Bill Bradley. *Sacred Hoops: : Spiritual Lessons of a Hardwood Warrior.* NY, NY: Hyperion, 1995.

Acknowledgements

There are several people who helped make this book a reality.

I owe a very special thank you to my wife, Melissa, who provided the encouragement to continue writing this book during the many times I thought about putting it aside. She also volunteered countless hours assisting with the project in various capacities. In addition to all of this, she continues be very supportive my racing "habit" as she calls it.

To my father, who brought me to many road racing events while growing up and even bought a go-cart for me to race around our backyard in as a child. In addition to continually providing support in many of my life's journeys, thank you both mom and dad, for taking the time and effort for the contributions you made to this book.

To Jake Fisher, a friend and fellow racer, who over long mountain bike rides had many discussions with me about the need for this type of book. Thank you for your added inspiration as well as other contributions to the book. (Oh, by the way, Jake is driving the MR2 on the book's front cover.)

To my uncle Rob Rarus for his editorial efforts. I appreciate the work and expertise you put into this project.

To Deb Stobbe, for allowing me to tap into her creativity. You continue to amaze me with the things you think of (almost all are good).

For all of the people who volunteer throughout club racing, without you, this type of racing would not be possible. You are sincerely appreciated and valued.

I also appreciate you taking the time to read this book and your help spreading the word about it.

Thank you

About the Author

Dave Gran was born on June 12, 1974 in Hartford, Connecticut. Even as a little child, he was always found running at full speed regardless of what he was doing. His passion for racing was fueled even greater by his father, Al Gran, who brought Dave to watch races at the local track, Lime Rock Park in CT. In 1997, Dave married his beautiful wife Melissa and continues to live in Connecticut.

In addition to his full-time banking career, he also instructs at high performance driving events with the Sports Car Drivers Association (www.SCDA1.com) and NASA. As a part-time job to help support his racing, he works for InControl ADT (www.InControlADT.com). The company primarily focuses on teaching teenage drivers advanced driving techniques.

Dave currently drives an ITB Honda Prelude Si.

Quick Order Form

Internet Orders: www.GoAheadTakeTheWheel.com
Postal Orders: Dragon Publishing
Suite 315
15 Oxford Drive
Newington, CT 06111

$16.95 US per copy
Sales tax: For books shipped to CT, add $1.26
Shipping: $5.00

Name: _____
Address: _____
Address: _____
City: _____
State: _____ Zip: _____
Telephone: _____
e-mail: _____

Total Amount Enclosed: $_____

Acceptable forms of payment: Money order, Cashier's check, or personal check. To pay by credit card, go to www.GoAheadTakeTheWheel.com. Please make check payable to Dragon Publishing.

Interested in selling or helping to promote this book at your shop or store? Contact us

Thank you for your order!